Cook Your Way to a Happy Ending

An Accumulation of Recipes Off the Beaten Path

by

Patric

AuthorHouse™
1663 Liberty Drive, Suite 200
Bloomington, IN 47403
www.authorhouse.com
Phone: 1-800-839-8640

First published by AuthorHouse 2/2/2009

ISBN: 978-1-4389-1788-7 (sc)

Printed in the United States of America
Bloomington, Indiana

This book is printed on acid-free paper.

Illustrated by Amanda Sandstrom

authorHOUSE®

To: Don & Heinrich
Double your Happy Endings!

Dedicated to Sterling....

For without you, we never would have laid on the floor and dreamed...

NOTE FROM DESIGNER: The image placements have shifted in the formatting between Mircosoft Word and InDesign. If there are any images that are missing, they should be resent to us in as a JPEG or TIF so that can be inserted where you'd like. If there's anything you don't like with the formatting (colors, photo placement, layout), we can make those changes free of charge.

ACKNOWLEDGEMENTS

So many people, so much talent. First to Gary who has never left my side and was willing to try something new, Paul for his unbelievable desire for the perfect Jello mold salad, Phil and his patience, Andrea, Alison(and the creamiest apple butter), Flora, Vinnie & Anna, Sara(the best photographer, ever), Grammie, George(for all I ever needed to know about sauerbraten). Brett, your technological knowledge, couldn't have done it without you. And for the countless wonders in the human spirit of good food I have yet to experience, thank you.

CONTENTS

APPETIZERS & STARTERS

CUMIN COCONUT SKEWERED CHICKEN

2 cloves garlic
3 tablespoon ground cumin
1 tablespoon chili powder
1 tablespoon ground coriander, or cup packed fresh cilantro
1 teaspoons paprika
1 cup coconut milk
1 teaspoon brown sugar
1 teaspoon salt
3 8 ounce chicken breasts, boneless, skinless
2 tablespoons vegetable oil
Skewers soaked in water for 1 hour

Combine the garlic, cumin, chili powder, coriander(cilantro), paprika, coconut milk, brown sugar and salt in a medium bowl. Slice each breast into ten strips. Thread each strip of chicken onto a skewer. Place the skewers in a shallow dish and pour marinade over. Cover and set aside, refrigerated for several hours, preferably overnight. In a large skillet, heat the oil and pan sear the chicken skewers for 4 to 6 minutes on each side until cooked through. Place skewers on cookies sheet and bake in preheated 400F degree oven for 8 to 10 minutes. Sprinkle with freshly ground black pepper to serve. Serves 30.

THE BEST CRAB CAKES

¼ cup mayonnaise
¼ cup minced red onion
2 large eggs, lightly beaten
½ teaspoon Worcestershire sauce
½ teaspoon dry mustard
¼ teaspoon salt
¼ teaspoon cayenne pepper
1 pound lump crab, or Dungeness crabmeat, picked over
1 cup soda crackers, finely crushed (or Panko)
2 tablespoons unsalted butter
½ cup vegetable oil

In a large bowl, combine the mayonnaise, onion, eggs, Worcestershire sauce, dry mustard, salt and cayenne. Fold in the crabmeat and ¼ cup of the cracker crumbs. Shape the mixture into 16 cakes and 1 inch thick. Coat the crab cakes with the remaining cracker crumbs and transfer to a baking sheet lined with waxed/parchment paper. The crab cakes can be refrigerated overnight at this point, if needed. In a large skillet, melt 1 tablespoon of the butter in 2 tablespoons of the oil. When the foam subsides, add half the crab cakes and cook over moderate heat until golden and crisp, 2 to 3 minutes per side. Drain on paper towels, then keep them warm in a low oven. Repeat with the remaining 1 tablespoon of butter and 2 tablespoons of oil and cook the remaining crab cakes. Serve with lemon wedges. Serves 8.

CROSTINI WITH ROASTED RED PEPPER, BRIE AND BASIL

1 large red bell pepper

4 ounces soft triple cream brie cheese room temperature about 1 cup

16 slices French baguette, oiled and lightly salted, grilled

16 fresh basil leaves

Preheat oven to 375° char bell pepper over gas flame or under broiler until blackened on all sides, enclose in paper bag 10 minutes peal and seed pepper cut into 1/2" wide strip's.

Spread brie cheese on toast topped with red pepper strips place crostini on baking sheet and bake until warm about five minutes top each toast with 2 basil leaves and serve. Serves 8

NAVY BEAN BRUSHETTA

3 ½ pounds navy beans, about 4 cups, cooked by manufacturers instructions,drained
2 garlic cloves smashed
2 teaspoons finely chopped thyme
2 teaspoons fresh lemon juice,
1 teaspoon finely grated lemon zest.
1 cup extra virgin olive oil, plus more for drizzling
salt and freshly ground pepper.
24, slices of Italian baguette
lime wedges for serving

Preheat the broiler. In a food processor, purée the beans with the garlic, thyme, lemon juice and lemon zest. With the machine on, add 3/4 cup of the olive oil in a thin stream and process until smooth. Scrape the navy bean purée into a medium bowl and season with salt and pepper. Brush the bread slices on both sides with remaining one quarter cup of olive oil. Arrange the slices on a baking sheet and broil about 4 inches from the heat for one minute per side, or until golden and crisp. Spread the toast with the navy bean purée and arrange the brushetta on a platter. Drizzle with the olive oil, sprinkle with salt and serve with lime wedges. Serves 24.

CRANBERRY ORANGE SALSA

12 ounces fresh cranberries, about 3 cups, coarsely chopped

½ cup honey, chestnut is best

2 medium and navel oranges, peeled sectioned and cut into 1/2" chunks

1 medium red grapefruit, peel, sectioned and cut into chunks

1 small red onion, finely chopped

½ cup dried apricots cut into thin strips

¼ to ½ cup minced fresh cilantro

1 to 2 habenero peppers seeded and minced

2 tablespoons lime juice

In a bowl, combine cranberries and honey. Stir in the oranges, grapefruit, onion, apricots, cilantro, habeneros, and lime juice. Cover and refrigerate for a least 2 hours.

BRANDIED MEATBALLS

2 pounds ground beef
¾ cup whole milk
½ cup bread crumbs, or Panko
1 tablespoon Worcestershire sauce
1 ½ teaspoons salt
1 teaspoon garlic powder
¼ teaspoon fresh ground nutmeg
¼ teaspoon ground ginger
¼ teaspoon freshly ground black pepper
Hot sauce to taste
Extra virgin olive oil
Brandied Peach Sauce
3 fresh peaches, sliced

Blend first 10 ingredients together in a bowl. Shape mixture into 1 ½ inch balls. In a large heavy skillet, brown meatballs in hot oil. Remove with a slotted spoon, set aside and keep warm. Reduce heat, lend Brandied Peach Sauce into meat drippings, and simmer for 10 minutes. Add meat balls to sauce and coat thoroughly. Cover and simmer for 45 minutes, cook over low heat until sauce is thickened. Transfer to serving platter and garnish with sliced peaches.

CEDAR PLANKED SALMON CHEESECAKE

3 tablespoons dried breadcrumbs, or Panko
5 tablespoons freshly grated Parmesan cheese, divided
½ cup chopped red onion
½ cup chopped yellow pepper
3 tablespoons unsalted butter
24 ounces cream cheese, softened
½ cup whipping cream, 40%
¼ teaspoon, fresh ground white pepper
4 extra large eggs
½ pound cedar planked salmon, flaked
½ cup shredded Manchego cheese

Grease the bottom and sides of a 9 inch springform pan. Combine the bread crumbs and 2 tablespoons Parmesan cheese; sprinkle into pan, coating bottom and sides. Set aside. In a skillet, sauté onion and yellow pepper in butter until tender; set aside. In a mixing bowl, beat cream cheese until fluffy. Beat in the cream, pepper and remaining Parmesan cheese. Add eggs; beat on low-speed, just until combined. Fold in the onion mixture, salmon and Manchego cheese. Wrap a double thickness of heavy-duty foil around the bottom of prepared and. Pour salmon mixture into pan. Place in a larger baking pan. Fill larger pan with hot water bath to a depth of 1 1/2". Bake at 325° for 35 to 40 minutes or until center is almost set. Cool on a wire rack for 1 hour. Refrigerate overnight. Remove foil and sides of pain and. Cut cheese cake into wedges; serve with crackers. Serves 14.

Cedar Planking is the process of cooking on a cedar board on an open flame or oven. Oil your fish and season with salt and pepper. Pre-soak your cedar for about 2 hours in water. Lay fish on board and put directly over high heat or in a moderately hot oven, 400F. Allow your cedar to smolder. Cook until just fish is just flakey, about 20 minutes.

SPICY POTATO CRISPS

4 medium unpeeled white baking potatoes
4 teaspoons salt, divided
4 cups ice water
1 tablespoon chili powder
1 teaspoon garlic salt
½ teaspoon cayenne pepper
½ teaspoon ground coriander
½ teaspoon ground cumin
oil for frying

Using a vegetable peeler or metal cheese slicer, cut potatoes into very thin lengthwise strips. Place in a large bowl; add 3 teaspoons salt and ice water. Soak for 30 minutes; drain. Place potatoes on paper towels and pat dry. In a bowl, combine the spices and remaining salt, set aside. Heat oil to 375°. Fry potatoes in oil in batches for 3 to 4 minutes or until deep golden brown, stirring frequently. Remove with a slotted spoon; drain on paper towels. Immediately sprinkle with the seasoning mixture. Store in airtight container. Serves 6.

RICOTTA AND ROASTED POBLANOS ON CUCUMBER

2 fresh poblano chilies
¾ cup whole milk fresh ricotta
¼ cup chopped scallions, green and white parts
2 tablespoons finely chopped fresh cilantro
¾ teaspoon kosher salt
English cucumber, sliced thin in rounds, skin intact
Finely diced pimiento

Lay chile's on their sides on rack of a gas burner and turned flame on high. Roast chiles, turning with tong's, until skins are blackened,5 to 8 minutes. Transfer chile is to a bowl and let stand, covered, 15 minutes. While chiles set, stir together ricotta, scallions, cilantro, and salt. Rub skins off chile's with paper towels and discard stems and seeds. Finely chop chiles and stir into ricotta mixture. Spoon some of the mixture onto the cucumber, garnish with finely diced pimiento. Serves 6.

HORSERADISH CRAB DIP

8 ounces cream cheese, softened
3 tablespoons picante sauce
2 tablespoons prepared horseradish
6 ounces lump crab meat, flaked
2 tablespoons grated lemon zest

In a mixing bowl, beat cream cheese, picante sauce, lemon zest and horseradish; mix well. Stir in the crab. Yield about 1 ½ cups.

OYSTER BIENVILLE

4 garlic cloves, peeled and minced
3 ribs celery, minced
2 medium red onion, peeled and minced
½ cup unsalted butter, melted
1 cup white flour
4 cups whole milk
1 ½ pounds cooked medium shrimp
½ cup sliced white mushrooms
1/3 cup dry white wine
½ cup minced Italian parsley
3 tablespoons minced chervil
Salt and freshly ground black pepper to taste
4 dozen oysters
Rock salt
Butter bread crumbs, or Panko
Pinch cayenne

In a heavy saucepan, sauté garlic, celery and onion in butter over moderate heat until tender. Reduce heat and gradually blend in flour and continue to cook for 3 minutes. Gradually add milk, mix well. Cook over moderate heat until thickened. Remove from heat and add shrimp, mushrooms, wine, parsley,and chervil. Season to taste. Spread rock salt in bottom of roasting pan. Arrange oysters on oiled half shell on salt. Spoon generous portion of mixture on oysters. Sprinkle with bread crumbs and pinch of cayenne pepper. Bake at 350F for 10 minutes. Serves 8.

SHRIMP LAYERED DEVILED EGGS

12 large eggs
1 tablespoon extra virgin olive oil
2/3 pound medium shrimp, shelled and deveined
salt and freshly ground black pepper
½ cup mayonnaise
¼ cup finely diced red radishes, about 4 large
2 tablespoons minced parsley
2 teaspoons capers, chopped
1 medium shallots, minced
1 garlic clove, minced

Put the eggs in a large saucepan and cover with cold water. Bring to a boil over moderate heat, then simmer the eggs over low heat for 10 minutes; drain. Transfer the eggs to a large bowl of ice water to chill thoroughly, then peel. Cut the eggs in half lengthwise. Put the yolks in a bowl and mashed lightly with a fork. Set the whites on a platter. Heat the olive oil in a large skillet. Add the shrimp, season with salt and pepper and cook over moderately high heat, stirring, until opaque, about 3 minutes. Transfer the shrimp to a work surface and cut 12 of them in half lengthwise cuts remaining shrimp into 1/3" dice. Add the diced shrimp to the egg yolks. Add the mayonnaise, radishes, parsley, capers, shallots and garlic, season with salt and pepper and stir to blend. Mound a rounded tablespoon of the filling in each egg white half and topped with a shrimp half. Serve at room temperature or chilled. Makes 2 dozen.

HERBED GOAT CHEESE SOUFFLES

1/3 pound full flavored, medium firm with goat cheese at room temperature
2 tablespoons milk
1 large egg yoke
fresh ground white pepper
2 teaspoons fresh finely chopped thyme
3 large egg whites at room temperature
Pinch of cream of tartar

Preheat the oven to 400°. Lightly oil 12- 1/4 cup ovenproof ramekins and arrange them on a small baking tray. Cut the rind off the cheese and discard. Crumble the cheese into a medium bowl. Beat the cheese and thyme with an electric mixer until fluffy. Add the egg, egg yolk and pepper and continue beating until the mixture is very thick and creamy. Wash and dry the beaters. In a medium bowl, beat the egg whites with the cream of tartar until stiff peaks form. Stir one fourth of the beaten egg whites into the cheese mixture to lighten it, then fold in the remaining whites. Spoon the soufflé mixture into the ramekins, mounting it in the center. Bake the soufflé is for 11 to 12 minutes, or until puffed and golden. Serve at once. Serves 12.

BACON WRAPPED STUFFED DATES WITH CUMIN HONEY

16 large Medjool dates, pitted

16 whole almonds

¼ cup mild goat cheese, crumbled

8 slices of bacon halved crosswise

Cumin honey(1 teaspoon ground cumin mixed with ½ cup chestnut honey)

Preheat the oven to 400°. Cut a lengthwise slit in the dates. Stuff each one with an almond and about one half teaspoon of the goat cheese. Pinch the dates closed. Wrap each date securely in a piece of bacon and arrange the dates, seeing side down, on a wire rack set on a baking sheet. Bake the stuffed dates for about 20 minutes, or until the bacon is brown and crisp; turn each date after 10 minutes. Drizzle cumin honey just before serving. Serve the stuffed dates warm or at room temperature.

SPICY MARGARITA SHRIMP

¼ cup, Juicy Margarita. (See recipe below)

2 tablespoons vegetable oil

1 chipotle in adobo, minced(for a wild ride, leave seeds)!

salt and freshly ground pepper

1 ½ pounds and medium shrimp, shelled and deveined, about 3 dozen shrimp

lime wedges, for serving

Preheat the broiler. In a glass bowl, mix the Juicy Margarita, oil and chipotle. Season with salt and pepper, add the shrimp and toss to coat. Let stand at room temperature for 15 minutes. Drain the shrimp and arrange them on a baking sheet. Broil the shrimp as close to the heat as possible for two to three minutes, turning once, until opaque and cooked through. Put 2 shrimp on each of 16 skewers and serve warm or at room temperature with lime wedges.

JUICY MARGARITA

1 cup tequila
$\frac{1}{2}$ cup Cointreau
1 $\frac{1}{4}$ cups fresh lime juice
$\frac{1}{4}$ cup fresh lemon juice
$\frac{1}{4}$ cup fresh orange juice
$\frac{1}{4}$ cup superfine sugar
4 teaspoons honey, warmed

Combine all of the ingredients and a large pitcher and stir to dissolve the sugar. Refrigerate until chilled.

CEDAR PLANKED SALMON WITH MUSTARD DILL SAUCE

One quarter cup corn oil
¼ cup honey mustard
4 teaspoons Dijon mustard
1 tablespoon sugar
2 teaspoons white wine vinegar
3 tablespoons chopped fresh dill
1 pound piece cedar planked salmon

Whisk first five ingredients in medium bowl to blend. Stir in dill. Season sauce to taste with salt and pepper. Can be prepared 2 days ahead. Cover and refrigerate. Serve salmon with sauce. Great with pumpernickel bread.

BLACK BEAN CAKES

2 – 15 ounce cans of black beans, drained well
6 green onions, finely chopped
½ cup finely chopped seeded red bell pepper
¼ cup chopped fresh cilantro
2 large garlic cloves, minced
1 ½ tablespoons minced seeded jalapeno chile
2 teaspoons ground cumin
2 teaspoons ground coriander
1 large egg
2 tablespoons plus 1 cup yellow cornmeal
6 tablespoons olive oil
sour cream
Cranberry Orange salsa

Place to drain beans in a large bowl. Using hand masher, mash beans coarsely. Mix green onions, bell pepper, cilantro,coriander, garlic, jalapeno and cumin. Season to taste with salt and pepper. Mix in egg and 2 tablespoons cornmeal. Place remaining 1 cup cornmeal in small dish. Drop heaping 1 tablespoon of bean mixture into cornmeal; turn to coat. Flatten into 1/2" thick cake. Repeat with remaining bean mixture and cornmeal, forming 18 cakes. Heat 3 tablespoons oil in heavy large skillet over medium heat. Working in batches, fry cakes until firm and crisp, adding more oil as needed, about 6 minutes per side. Drain bean cakes on paper towels. Serve warm with sour cream and salsa.

MOZZARELLA TART WITH SWEET SAUSAGE

One piecrust, prepard
½ pound sweet sausages, casings removed
¾ cup grated mozzarella cheese, about 3 ounces
2/3 cup diced salami
½ cup grated Parmesan cheese
¼ cup chopped fresh basil
4 extra large eggs
½ cup whole milk
1/8 teaspoon fresh ground nutmeg

Preheat oven to 425°. Unfold crusts on work surface, pressed together any cracks in dough to seal crust. Place crust in 9 inch diameter tart pan with removable bottom; fold in excess dough and press, forming double thick sides that extend about 1/4" above the rim of pan. Pierce crust with fork. Bake crust 5 minutes cut; press with back a fork if crust bubbles up. Continue to bake until crust is golden brown, about 10 minutes. Set aside. Reduce oven temperature to 425°. Meanwhile, sauté sausages in heavy medium skillet over medium-high heat until brown, breaking into small pieces with back of fork, about 6 minutes. Using slotted spoon, transfer sausage to large bowl; cool. Add mozzarella, salami, parmesan and basil. Toss sausage mixture to blend. Spoon sausage mixture into prepared crust. Beat eggs, milk and not make in medium bowl to blend; season with pepper. Pour custard over sausage mixture in crust. Bake tart until filling is set in center and golden brown on top, about 25 minutes. Let cool 10 minutes and serve. Cut into slim wedges for an appetizer or first course, serving on a bed of Bibb lettuce. Serves 10.

EMPANADAS WITH ALMOND CURRY RICE

1 cup white rice
¼ cup unsalted butter
1 red onion, minced
1 green bell pepper, minced
½ cup slivered almonds, toasted
1 cup gold raisins
2 cups chicken stock
1 teaspoon curry powder
1 teaspoon orange zest
2 tablespoon Majoy Greys Chutney
1 tablespoon pimiento, chopped

Saute rice in butter until white. Add seasoning, vegetables and liquid. Cover after coming to a boil. Cook over low heat for 45 minutes, or until liquid is absorbed. Add chutney and toasted almonds. Cut puff pastry to 2 inch rounds and place 1 teaspoon of rice on top. Fold over in half and seal. Press lightly with fork to complete. Bake in preheated 400F oven for 20 minutes or until golden and puffed. Yields 24 empanadas.

SALADS

BEET, JICAMA AND GINGER SALAD

2 pounds medium beats
2 pounds jicama, julienned
¼ cup sherry wine vinegar
1 tablespoon plus 1 teaspoon minced fresh ginger
salt and freshly ground pepper
3 tablespoons of vegetable oil
4 chives cut into 2 inch lengths

Preheat the oven to 350°. Wash the beats and while still wet, wrap them individually in foil. Set them on a baking sheet and bake for one hour and 15 minutes, or until fork tender when pierced. Rub the skins off the warm beats under cold running water. Slice the beets crosswise 1/4" thick, then stack the slices and cut them into 1/4" strips. In a medium bowl, mix the vinegar jicama and ginger. Season with salt and pepper. Slowly whisk in the oil, to emulsify. Add the beats, toss to coat and let marinate for at least 30 minutes. Garnish with the chives and serve at room temperature.

SHAVED FENNEL, BOK CHOY AND POMEGRANATE SALAD

Vinaigrette:
1tablespoon raspberry vinegar
½ teaspoon Dijon mustard
1½ teaspoons chopped fresh tarragon
1/8 teaspoon salt
1/8 teaspoon freshly ground black pepper
3 tablespoons extra virgin olive oil

6 cups spring mix lettuces
1 1/3 cups shaped fennel
1 large head bok choy, chopped in 1 inch pieces, root included
seeds from one pomegranate, about 11/2 cups
¼ cup toasted sliced almonds

In a small bowl, whisk together vinegar, mustard, tarragon, salt and pepper. Slowly whisk in oil until blended. When ready to serve, in a large bowl, toss lettuce with vinaigrette. Divide lettuce among 4 salad plates. Sprinkle with fennel, bok choy, pomegranate and toasted almonds. Serves 4.

ARTICHOKE SALAD WITH ORANGE VINIAGRETTE

One lemon, halved
3 large artichokes
2 tablespoons extra virgin olive oil
2 slices bacon, cut into 1 inch pieces
2 garlic cloves, thinly sliced one carrot, thinly sliced
1 medium onion, thinly sliced
2 cups dry Riesling wine
1 cup water
2 thyme sprigs
1 bay leaf
salt and freshly ground pepper
2 teaspoons fresh orange zest
½ teaspoon sherry vinegar
½ teaspoon fresh orange juice
1 head Bibb lettuce, leaves separated

Squeeze the lemon juice into a bowl of cold water; add the lemon to the bowl. Using a sharp stainless steel knife, cut off the artichokes stems and halve the artichokes crosswise. Discard the tops. Working with one artichoke at a time, pull off the outer green leaves from the bottoms until you reach the yellow leaves. Trim off the tough outer skin. Scrape out the hairy choke with a teaspoon, then drop the artichoke hearts into the lemon water. Heat ½ tablespoons of the olive oil in a medium saucepan.

Add the bacon and cook over low heat, stirring until the fat begins to melt, about 4 minutes. Stir in the garlic, carrot and onion. Cover and cook over low heat until the vegetables are softened, about 8 minutes.

Add the remaining 1 1/2 tablespoons of olive oil, and the artichoke hearts. Stir in the Riesling wine, water, thyme and bay leaf and bring to a boil. Season with salt and pepper and simmer over low heat until the artichoke hearts are tender, about 15 minutes. Using a slotted spoon, transfer the artichoke hearts to a plate. Skim 1 1/2 tablespoons of oil from the artichoke broth and put the oil in a small bowl. Crumble the saffron threads into the oil. Strain the artichoke broth. Pour ½ cup of the broth into the saucepan and boil over high heat until reduced by half, about 3 minutes. Discard any remaining artichoke broth. Cut one artichoke heart in half and cut one of the halves into chunks. Transfer the artichoke chunks to a blender. Add the reduced broth and purée. With the machine on, slowly add the saffron oil and blend until smooth. Scrape the purée into a small bowl and stir in the sherry vinegar and lemon juice. Season with salt and pepper. Thinly slice the remaining 2 ½ artichoke hearts. In a medium bowl, toss the lettuce with one tablespoon of the vinaigrette and arrange it on 2 plates. Top the Bibb lettuce with the sliced artichokes and drizzle with the remaining saffron vinaigrette and serve.

WHITE CORN AND CELERY SLAW WITH EDAMAME

4 large tender celery ribs, plus 2 tablespoons coarsely chopped celery leaves

2 cups, frozen edamame in their pods

2 cups fresh white corn kernels

2 scallions, white and tender green parts, thinly sliced on the diagonal

1/4 cup cilantro leaves

1 tablespoon torn minced leaves

1 tablespoon fresh lime juice

1 tablespoon canola oil

In a food processor or with a sharp knife, sliced the celery as thinly as possible. In a medium saucepan of boiling water, cook the soybeans 45 minutes. Drain and refresh under cold water. Shell the soybeans and pat dry. Add the soybeans,corn, salt, cilantro, scallions, minced and celery leaves to the salary and toss well. In a bowl, whisk the lime juice with the oil. Pour the dressing over the vegetables, season with salt, toss and serve. Serves 4.

MIXED RICE SALAD

3 ½ cups vegetable stock
1 tablespoon light soy sauce
1 tablespoon unsolphured molasses
½ cup black rice
2 tablespoons extra virgin olive oil
½ cup brown rice
15 ounces chickpeas
½ red onion, diced
1 bell pepper, diced
3 ounces rehydrated apricots, sliced
½ cup golden raisins
2 tablespoons cilantro
½ cup sliced toasted almonds

Dressing:
1 teaspoon curry
1 teaspoon coriander
1 teaspoon turmeric
1 teaspoon nutmeg
½ teaspoon cayenne pepper
¼ cup rice vinegar
2 tablespoons honey
1 tablespoon fresh squeezed lemon juice
1/3 cup extra virgin olive oil

Put 1 ½ cups stock, soy sauce and molasses and saucepan, bring to boil. Add rice and bring back to boil. Cover and simmer gently for 50 minutes, remove from heat and cool. Heat the oil, add brown rice and stir for about 2 minutes to coat with oil. Add remaining stock and bring to boil: reduce heat to low and simmer covered tightly, for about 40 minutes until stock is absorbed. Remove from the heat and cool slightly. Meanwhile, make the dressing. Heat all spices in a dry pan, cool, whisk vinegar, honey and lemon juice in a large bowl. Add oil, whisk in cooled spice mixture. Fork rice into dressing and mix well. Stir in chickpeas, onion, bell pepper, apricots, raisins, and cilantro. Sprinkle with the sliced toasted almonds. Serves 6.

GREEN BEAN AND ONION WITH WARM CIDER VINIAGRETTE

½ cup frozen apple juice concentrate, thawed
2 tablespoons apple cider vinegar
2 tablespoons vegetable oil
2 teaspoons Dijon mustard
1 teaspoon mustard seeds

6 ounces green beans, trimmed, cut in half on deep diagonal
4 cups packed baby greens
½ cup finely chopped red onion
2 large radishes, trimmed, halved, thinly sliced
1 tablespoon finely chopped bread and butter pickles

Boil apple concentrate in small saucepan over medium heat until reduced to ¼ cup, about 5 minutes. Remove from the heat. Whisk in vinegar, oil, mustard and mustard seeds. Season vinaigrette with salt and pepper. Cook beans in medium pot of boiling salted water until crisp tender, about 4 minutes; drain well. Transfer beans to large bowl; cool slightly. Add greens, onion, radishes and pickles. Toss with enough vinaigrette to coat.

WILTED ARUGULA WITH CURRIED CROUTONS

1 head of garlic
4 tablespoons plus ¾ cup olive oil
¼ cup finely chopped shallots
4 tablespoons balsamic vinegar
2 tablespoons chopped fresh thyme
2 large red onions, sliced into 1/4″ thick rings, separated
2 tablespoons butter, ¼ stick
6 garlic cloves, chopped
1 teaspoon curry powder
2 cups 1/2″ cubes day-old ciabatta bread
1 teaspoon chopped fresh rosemary
8 cups packed arugula leaves
1 cup packed grated mozzarella cheese, about 4 ounces

For the vinaigrette:
Preheat oven to 350°. Place garlic in small baking dish. Drizzle with 2 tablespoons oil. Cover dish tightly with foil; bake until garlic is tender, about 15 minutes. Cool. Squeeze roasted garlic from skins into medium bowl. Mash with fork. Add ¾ cup oil, shallots,3 tablespoons vinegar and thyme. Whisk to blend well. Season with salt and pepper. Increase oven temperature to 375°. Oil large rimmed baking sheet. Arrange onion rings on sheet. Sprinkle with salt and pepper. Drizzle with remaining 2 tablespoons oil; toss to coat and roast until tender and brown, stirring occasionally, about 30 minutes. Drizzle with remaining one tablespoon vinegar; toss to coat. Add onions to vinaigrette in bowl, maintain oven temperature.

For the salad:
Melt butter in heavy medium ovenproof skillet over medium heat. Add chopped garlic and curry, sauté 30 seconds. Add bread cubes and rosemary and toss to combine. Transfer to oven and bake until croutons are golden and crisp, about 10 minutes. Place arugula in large bowl. Add cheese and toss to combine. Transfer vinaigrette to medium saucepan. Stir over medium low heat until hot. Pour hot dressing over arugula salad and toss to combine.

COUSCOUS WITH SHRIMP AND ALMONDS

3 cups vanilla yogurt
1 1/2 cups extra virgin olive oil
2 tablespoons ground cumin
6 tablespoons fresh lemon juice
2 garlic cloves, pressed
6 cups water
1/4 teaspoon salt
3-10 ounce packages plain couscous
8 tangerines, peeled, seeded, cut into 1/4" pieces, about 4 cups
2-15 ounce cans garbanzo beans, drained
1 cup golden raisins
2 pounds cooked peeled deveined large shrimp, about 50, halved lengthwise
1 cup finely chopped green onions
1 cup sliced almonds, toasted

Place yogurt in medium bowl. Gradually whisk in oil and cumin. Stir in lemon juice and garlic. Season dressing to taste with salt and pepper. Cover and chill. Note: may be made two days ahead. Keep refrigerated. Mix 6 cups water and salt in large saucepan; bring to boil. Mix in couscous. Remove from heat. Cover; let stand until water is absorbed in couscous is tender, about 10 minutes. Transfer couscous to large bowl; fluff with fork. Cool to room temperature. Gently mix in tangerines, garbanzo beans, raisins, 3/4 of shrimp, ¾ cup green onions and ½ cup almonds. Season salad to taste with salt and pepper. Note: can be made four hours ahead. Cover; chill. Let stand at room temperature 30 minutes before serving. Garnish with remaining shrimp, green onions and almonds.

JICAMA GINGER SLAW

2 cups julienned jicama

2 cups julienned carrots

2 cup julienned cucumber, skin on

2 red bell peppers, seeded, cut into match stick size strips

¼ cup finely sliced fresh ginger

½ cup rice wine vinegar

1 tablespoon sugar

2 teaspoons packed grated lemon zest

Toss jicama, carrots,cucumbers, red bell peppers and fresh ginger in large bowl to combine. Whisk rice vinegar, sugar and grated lemon peel in small bowl to blend. Pour dressing over vegetables and toss to combine. Season slaw to taste with salt and pepper. Let stand at least 20 minutes, drain before serving.

APPLES, AVOCADO AND BACON
with SPINACH AND FETA

1 cup extra virgin olive oil
¼ cup powdered sugar
¼ cup apple cider vinegar
1 tablespoon fresh squeezed lemon juice
1 ½ teaspoon dry mustard
1 ½ teaspoons paprika
½ teaspoon fresh ground ginger
½ pound applewood smoked bacon slices, chopped
2-6 ounce bags baby spinach leaves washed and dried
2 medium sized apples halved, thinly sliced, tart apple work nicely
1 cup very thinly sliced red onion
1 ripe avocado, halved, pitted, peeled, cubed
1 cup feta cheese, crumbled

Whisk oil, powdered sugar, vinegar, lemon juice, dry mustard, paprika and ground ginger in small bowl to blend. Season to taste with salt and pepper. Sauté chopped the bacon slices in heavy large skillet over medium-high heat until brown and crisp. Using slotted spoon, transfer chopped bacon to paper towel and drain. Combine baby spinach leaves apple slices, red onion, avocado and bacon in large bowl. Toss salad with enough dressing to coat. Garnish with feta.

MIXED GREENS WITH PUMPKIN SEEDS AND ASIAGO CHEESE

6 tablespoons apple cider vinegar
1 shallot, minced
1 teaspoon Dijon mustard
1 teaspoon honey
¾ cup extra virgin olive oil
1 large head red leaf lettuce, torn into bite size pieces
1large head butter lettuce, torn into bite size pieces
3 bunches watercress, trimmed
3/4 cup roasted salted pumpkin seeds
1 piece Asiago cheese

Whisk first of four ingredients in small bowl to blend. Gradually whisk in oil. Season to taste with salt and pepper. Combine lettuces and watercress in large bowl. Add dressing and toss to coat. Sprinkle with pumpkin seeds. Grate cheese on salads and serve.

STRAWBERRIES WITH ROASTED PEPPERS AND PINENUTS

6 large red bell peppers, halved, seeded
6 large yellow bell peppers, halved, seeded
6 large orange bell peppers, halved, seeded
8 tablespoons extra virgin olive oil
3 tablespoon, or more, balsamic vinegar
½ cup pine nuts, toasted
2 cups sliced stawberries

Preheat oven to 400°. Place all bell peppers in large bowl. Pour six tablespoons oil over peppers; toss to coat. Place peppers, cut side down, on two large rimmed baking sheet. Sprinkle with salt. Roast until peppers are soft and slightly blackened, about one hour, reversing sheets after 30 minutes. Cool slightly; peel, if desired. Cut peppers into 1/4" wide strips. Transfer to large bowl; add accumulated juices from baking sheets. Add three tablespoons vinegar and remaining two tablespoons oil; toss gently. Refrigerate at least one hour. Drain peppers; discard juices. Transfer peppers to platter. Season with salt and pepper and more vinegar, if desired. Sprinkle with toasted pine nuts and a generous handful of sliced strawberries.

MUSHROOM SALAD

3 pounds and medium white mushrooms, trimmed and quartered
3 tablespoons fresh squeezed lemon juice
2 tablespoons unsalted butter
2 tablespoons plus 1 teaspoon pure extra virgin olive oil
2 tablespoons sherry vinegar
2 tablespoons Marsala
2 teaspoons tomato paste
1 tablespoon soy sauce
salt and freshly ground pepper
2 garlic cloves, minced
3 large shallots, thinly sliced
6 cups coarsely shredded Romaine lettuce
2 cups coarsely shredded Boston lettuce
½ cup shredded Gouda cheese, aged Gouda or goat Gouda

In a large bowl, toss the mushrooms with the lemon juice. Preheat the oven to 300°. In a large skillet, melt the butter in 2 tablespoons of the pure olive oil over moderately high heat. When the butter starts to brown, add the mushrooms and season with salt and pepper. Cover and cook until the mushrooms release their liquid, about 3 minutes. Uncover and cook, stirring occasionally, until the liquid has evaporated and the mushrooms are deeply browned, about 8 minutes. Add the soy sauce and cook, stirring, for 2 minutes longer. Transfer the mushrooms to a rimmed baking sheet and keep warm in the oven. In a small bowl, whisk the extra virgin olive oil with the sherry vinegar, Marsala, tomato paste and minced garlic. Season the sherry vinegar with salt and pepper. Add the remaining 1 teaspoon of pure olive oil to the skillet. Add the shallots, cover and cook over moderately high heat until softened, about 3 minutes. Uncover and cook, stirring, until lightly browned. Stir in the sherry vinegar and remove from the heat. In a bowl, toss the lettuces. Add the mushrooms and shallots and toss well. Arrange the salad, sprinkle with the cheese and serve at once.

HARICOTS VERTS WITH SCALLOPS AND WHITE TRUFFLE OIL

3 tablespoons sherry wine vinegar
1 ½ tablespoons minced shallots
2 ½ tablespoons canola oil
6 ounces haricots verts, or other slender green bean, trimmed, cut into 2 inch lengths
2 small heads Belgian endive, thinly sliced on diagonal
6 sea scallops, about 10 ounces, 1 teaspoon curry powder
2 teaspoons white truffle oil
¼ cup chopped fresh chives
¼ cup chopped terragon

Combine vinegar and shallot in small bowl. Whisk in 1½ tablespoons canola oil. Season vinaigrette with salt and pepper. Cook haricot verts in medium pot of boiling salted water until just tender, about 4 minutes. Drain. Refresh under cold running water. Drain. Mix and add 2 tablespoons vinaigrette in medium bowl; toss to combine. Let stand 20 minutes. Keep remaining one tablespoon canola oil in heavy large skillet over medium heat. Sprinkle scallops with curry powder. Add to skillet and cook 3 minutes; turn over and cook until almost opaque in center, about 2 minutes longer. Place three scallops around boarder of each plate. Using half of haricot verts for each plate, place three small bundles of haricots verts between scallops. Mound half of the endive mixture in center of each plate. Drizzle remaining vinaigrette over haricots verts and scallops. Drizzle 1 teaspoon truffle over each salad. Sprinkle salad with tarragon and chives.

BLACK EYED PEAS WITH GARLIC AND LEMON

2 ½ cups dried black-eyed peas, 1 pound, soaked overnight and drained
¼ cup plus two tablespoons extra virgin olive oil
¼ cup fresh lemon juice
2 tablespoons fresh lemon zest
2 teaspoons minced garlic
1 large onion, finely chopped
salt and freshly ground pepper
¼ cup finely chopped flat leaf parsley

In a large saucepan, cover the black-eyed peas with 2 inches of water. Bring to a boil, cover partially and cook over moderately low heat until tender, about 20 minutes. Drain and let cool slightly. In a large bowl, whisk the olive oil with the lemon juice and garlic. Add the peas and onion and season with salt and pepper, then toss to coat. Refrigerate for at least 4 hours to let the flavors blend. Bring the salad to room temperature, stir in the parsley and serve.

ROCKET WITH GOAT CHEESE AND DRIED APRICOTS

1 teaspoon unsalted butter
1/3 cup sliced almonds
2 tablespoons extra virgin olive oil
2 tablespoons balsamic vinegar
salt and freshly ground pepper
10 ounces rocket, or arugula
½ cup dried apricots
4 ounces mild goat cheese, crumbled

Melt the butter in a small skillet. Add the almonds and cook over moderately high heat, stirring constantly, until golden, about three minutes. Drain on paper towels and let cool completely. In a small bowl, whisk the olive oil with the vinegar and season the vinaigrette with salt and pepper. In a large bowl, toss the rocket with apricots and almonds. Add the vinaigrette and toss well. Add the goat cheese, toss the salad lightly and serve.

GINGER, GREEN APPLE, SWEET ONION AND COCONUT SALAD

2 Granny Smith apples, julienned
1 small sweet onion, such as the Vidalia, julienned
1 3- inch piece of ginger, peeled and julienned
½ cup finely freshly grated coconut
3 tablespoons fresh squeezed lemon juice
2 tablespoons finely shredded fresh basil
salt and freshly ground pepper
lemon verbena oil (recipe next page)

Toss the apples with the onion, ginger, coconut, lemon juice and fresh basil. Season with salt and pepper. Add 3 tablespoons of lemon verbena oil and toss; serve.

LEMON VERBENA OIL

1 cup lemon verbena leaves, about 3 ounces, or 2 stalks fresh lemon grass, tender inner white bulbs only, crushed

½ cup grapeseed oil

pinch of salt

In a blender, combine the lemon verbena with the oil and blend for 2 minutes. Pour the oil into a jar and let stand for one hour, then strain, pressing on the solids to extract as much oil as possible. Season with salt.

SUGAR SNAP PEA AND PROSCIUTTO SALAD

¾ pound sugarsnap peas
3 tablespoons extra virgin olive oil
1 teaspoon finely grated lemon zest
1 ½ tablespoons fresh squeezed lemon juice
3 tablespoons finely chopped chocolate basil
3 ounces and thinly sliced prosciutto, cut into thin strips, fat removed
salt and freshly ground pepper

Blanch the sugar snap peas in a medium saucepan of boiling salted water until crisp tender, about one minute. Drain and plunge into an ice bath. Pat the sugar snaps dried. In a medium bowl, whisk the olive oil, lemon zest, lemon juice and basil. Add the sugar snaps and prosciutto, season with salt and pepper and toss.

SHIRMP SALAD WITH WATERCRESS, CANNELLINI AND MINT

1 pound large shrimp, shelled and deveined

5 1/2 tablespoons extra virgin olive oil

salt and freshly ground pepper

1/4 cup packed fresh mint leaves, washed thoroughly to remove sand

2 tablespoons warm water

1 15 ounce can cannellini beans, drained and rinsed

1 tablespoon fresh squeezed lemon juice

1 bunch watercress, tough stems discarded

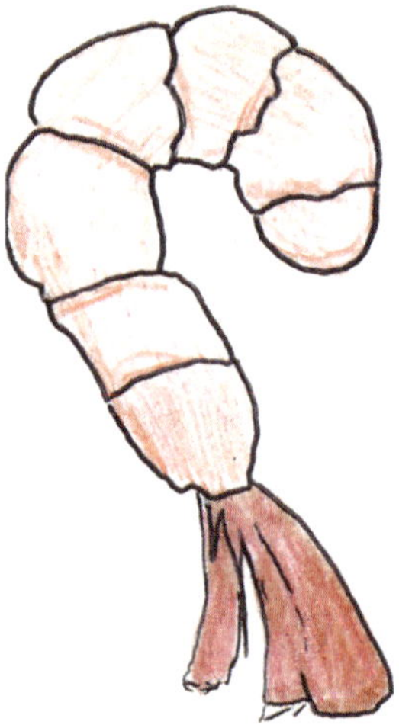

Preheat the broiler and position a rack 6 inches from the heat. Toss the shrimp with 1 tablespoon of the olive oil and season with salt and pepper. Broil the shrimp for 3 minutes, turning once, until opaque throughout. In a food processor, pulse the mint with the warm water. Add 4 tablespoons of the olive oil and purée until smooth. In a medium bowl, toss the beans with the mint oil and shrimp and season with salt and pepper. In a large bowl, whisk the lemon juice with remaining 1/2 tablespoon of olive oil. Add the watercress, season with salt and pepper and toss gently. Mound the watercress on a plate and spoon the shrimp salad on top. Serve with lemon wedges.

NASTURTIUM AND SPROUT SALAD

¼ pound mixed sprouts, such as alfalfa, watercress, broco sprouts, about 4 cups
1 Granny Smith apple, finely julienned
1 ½ teaspoon toasted peanut or sesame oil
1 ½ teaspoons sunflower oil
fine seasalt
large nasturtium leaves
½ cup plain yogurt

In a large bowl, toss the sprouts with the apple, peanut oil and sunflower oil. Season with salt. Mound 1/2 cup of the sprouts salad on each plate, divide by four. Top each mound with a nasturtium leaf and remaining salad. Drizzle the yogurt around the plate and serve.

CITRUS SPINACH SALAD

3 tablespoons clover honey
2 tablespoons fresh squeezed lime juice
1 teaspoon grated fresh lime zest
1/8 to 1/4 teaspoon freshly grated nutmeg
1/3 cup vegetable oil
10 cups fresh spinach
3 medium navel oranges, peeled and sectioned
2 medium pink grapefruit, peeled and sectioned
1 medium red onion, sliced and separated into rings

In a food processor, combine the honey, lime juice, line zest and nutmeg; process until blended. While processing, gradually add oil in a steady stream until dressing is thickened and emulsified. In a large bowl, combine the spinach, oranges and grapefruit. Drizzle with dressing; toss to coat. Top with onion. Serves 12.

CARPACCIO WITH ROASTED CIPOLLINI AND GOAT CHEESE

1 cup extra virgin olive oil
5 tablespoons red wine vinegar
2 tablespoons fresh thyme leaves
2 large garlic cloves
1 ½ pound beef tenderloin, sliced tissue thin
18 cipollini onions, roasted
8 cups mixed salad greens
1 cup crumbled chilled soft fresh goat cheese, about 4 ounces

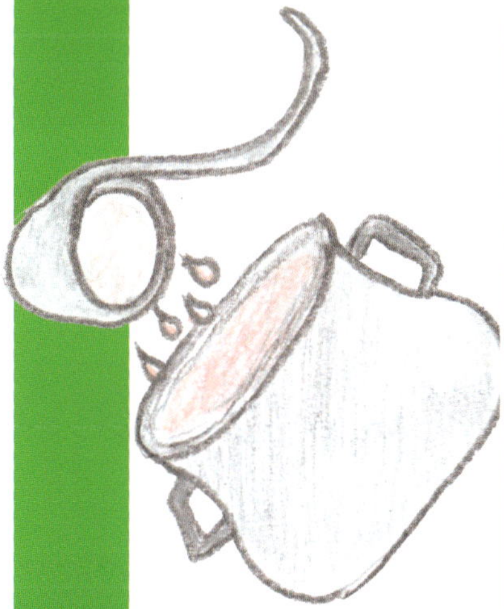

Blend oil, vinegar, thyme and garlic in food processor until garlic is chopped; season dressing with salt and pepper. Place beef in glass baking dish. Add 1/3 cup dressing; turn to coat. Cover and chill 30 minutes. Meanwhile, preheat oven to 450°. Toss shallots and 2 tablespoons dressing on baking sheet to coat. Roast onions until caramelized and tender, stirring occasionally, about 20 minutes; set aside. Place greens and shallots and large bowl; toss with enough dressing to coat. Mound greens on large platter. Surrounded with carpaccio; sprinkle with goat cheese. Serves 4.

SOUPS

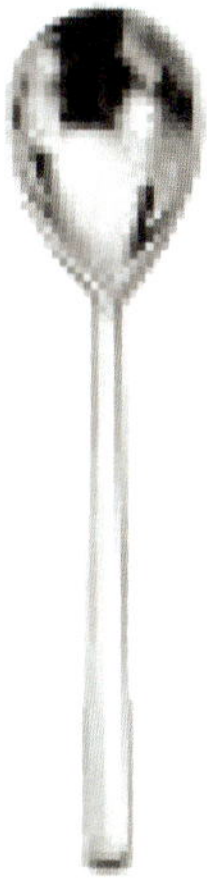

TWO BEAN MINESTRONE WITH PANCETTA AND PARMESAN

½ cup dried chickpeas, about 4 ounces, soaked overnight and drained
1 quart water
½ cup dried Pinto beans, about 3 ounces, soaked overnight and drained
2 tablespoons extra virgin olive oil
5 ounces pancetta, finely chopped
1 large onion, coarsely chopped
1 medium leek, white and tender green parts, coarsely chopped
4 large garlic cloves, minced
2 large celery ribs, finely chopped
2 medium carrots, finely chopped
8 cups chicken stock
4 thyme sprigs and 2 bay leaves
2 sage sprigs
13 ounce piece of Parmesan rind
¼ pound Savoy cabbage, coarsely chopped, 4 cups
½ pound kale, large stems discarded, leaves finely chopped, 5 cups
1/2 cups canned peeled Italian tomatoes, coarsely chopped, juices reserved
½ pound green beans, cut into 1 inch lengths
salt and freshly ground pepper

In a medium saucepan, cover the chickpeas with the water and bring to a boil. Reduce the heat to low, cover and simmer for 30 minutes. Add the Pinto beans, cover and continue to simmer until the beans are tender, about 1 hour. Remove from the heat and set the beans aside. Meanwhile, keep the olive oil in a large enameled cast iron casserole. Add the pancetta and cook over low heat until golden, about 5 minutes. Add the onion, leek, garlic, celery and carrots and cook, stirring, for 3 minutes. Add the stock, thyme, bay leaves, sage and Parmesan rind and simmer for 5 minutes. Add the cabbage, kale, tomatoes and their juices and cooked beans and their liquid. Cover and simmer for 45 minutes. Add the green beans, cover and continue to simmer for 1 hour. Discard the thyme sprigs, bay leaves, sage and Parmesan rind. Season with salt and pepper and remove from the heat. Serves

ROASTED CORN SOUP WITH ROSEMARY

2 cups chopped red onion
½ cup diced carrots
½ cup diced celery
3 tablespoons unsalted butter, divided
6 cups chicken stock
7 cups roasted corn with any liquid reserved
1 tablespoon minced fresh rosemary, crushed
2 large garlic cloves, minced
¼ teaspoon cayenne pepper
1 medium sweet red pepper, chopped
1 cup heavy cream, 40%
salt and freshly ground black pepper

In a large saucepan sauté onions, carrots and celery in 2 tablespoons butter until tender. Add 4 cups corn, stock, rosemary, garlic and cayenne. Bring to a boil. Reduce heat; simmer, uncovered, for 30 minutes, stirring occasionally. Cool; process in batches in a food processor until puréed. Return to the pan. In a small skillet, sauté red pepper in remaining butter until tender. Add to corn mixture. Stir in cream and remaining corn; keep through, stirring occasionally. Season to taste with salt and pepper. Serves 8.

LEEK AND CAULIFLOWER VISCHYSOISE WITH OYSTERS

2 tablespoons unsalted butter

2 large leeks, whites and tender green parts, thinly sliced

1 - 2 pound cauliflower, cut into large florettes

6 cups water

1/3 cup crème fraîche

salt and freshly ground white pepper

2 tablespoons finely diced peeled English cucumber

2 tablespoons minced chives

1tablespoon minced shallot

1 tablespoon rice wine vinegar

1 tablespoon extra virgin olive oil

4 oysters, shucked

Melt the butter in a large saucepan. Add the leeks and cook over low heat until tender, about 8 minutes. Add the cauliflower and water and bring to a boil. Simmer over low heat until the cauliflower is soft, about 35 minutes. Add the crème fraîche, bring back to a simmer and remove from the heat. Purée the soup in a food processor in batches until very smooth. Season with salt and white pepper and chill thoroughly. Just before serving, combine the cucumber, chives, shallots, vinegar and olive oil in a small bowl. Ladle the cold soup into for shallow bowls and spoon and oyster onto the center of each. Spoon the cucumber mixture around the oysters. Serves 4.

SAGE INFUSED HERB SOUP

2 tablespoons unsalted butter
2 large shallots, minced
2 small red potatoes, peeled and halved
2 medium carrots, cut into sticks
1 ½ quart chicken stock
2 cups at flat leaf parsley leaves
1 cup basil leaves
½ cup fresh cilantro leaves
2 tablespoons tarragon leaves
1 tablespoon fresh sage leaves, minced
1 tablespoon fresh lemon juice
salt and freshly ground pepper
crême fraîche, for garnish

Melt the butter in a large saucepan. Add the shallots and cook over low heat until softened, about 5 minutes. Add the potatoes, carrots and chicken stock and bring to a boil. Cover and simmer over low heat until the vegetables are tender, about 10 minutes. Add the parsley, basil, cilantro, terragon and sage to the soup. Working in batches, purée the soup in a blender. Return the soup to the saucepan, add the lemon juice and season with salt and pepper. Spoon dollop of crème fraiche when serving.

TRI-MUSHROOM SOUP WITH BRIE CROUTONS

¼ cup, (1/2 stick), butter, unsalted
3 large leeks, white and pale green parts only, thinly sliced
8 ounces oyster mushrooms, sliced
8 ounces shiitake mushrooms, stemmed, sliced
8 ounces crimini mushrooms, sliced
2 tablespoons all-purpose flour
4 cups chicken stock
1 cup whipping cream, 40%
2 tablespoons dry sherry
4 green onions, sliced

12 1/4" thick slices French bread baguette
½ pound brie, frozen, rind removed, cut into 1/4" thick slices

2 tablespoons chopped fresh chives

Melt butter in large pot over medium-high heat. Add leeks and all mushrooms; sauté 8 minutes. Add flour and stir 1 minute. Gradually mix in stock. Bring to boil, stirring frequently. Reduce heat and simmer 10 minutes. Add cream and sherry and simmer five minutes. Season to taste with salt and pepper. Stir in green onions. Preheat oven to 350°. Place bread slices on baking sheet. Bake until light golden, about 10 minutes. Cool. Top croutons with cheese slices. Preheat broiler. Place 6 ovenproof bowls on baking sheet. Bring soup to a simmer; ladle into bowls. Top each with two croutons. Broil until cheese is completely melted, about 2 minutes. Sprinkle with chives and serve. Serves 6.

CURRIED APPLE ZUCCHINI SOUP

2 tablespoons butter, unsalted
1 large onion, chopped
1 large apple, peeled, cord and chopped
1- 2 teaspoons curry powder
1 quart chicken stock
2 cups diced zucchini
¼ cup uncooked white rice
½ teaspoons salt
1 cup whole milk, or cream

In a saucepan, melt the butter and sauté the onions and apples until soft. Sprinkle with the curry powder and cook, stirring, for about one minute. Pour in the stock and bring to a boil. Add the zucchini, rice and salt and cook until zucchini is tender, about 30 minutes. Cool slightly and pour into a blender or food processor and purée until smooth. Return to the saucepan, add the milk or cream and heat, do not boil. Serves 4 to 6.

BLEU CHEESE ARTICHOKE SOUP

1 tablespoon unsalted butter
1 medium onion, chopped
1/3 cup dry sherry
16 ounces artichoke hearts
3 cups chicken broth
2 tablespoons fresh thyme
¼ cup heavy cream, 40%
¼ cup crumbled blue cheese
chopped fresh chives

Melt butter in heavy large saucepan over medium heat. Add onion and sauté until translucent, about 10 minutes. Add sherry and simmer until all liquid evaporates, about 4 minutes. Add artichokes, broth, and thyme. Simmer until artichoke hearts began to fall apart, about 10 minutes. Remove from heat. Cool slightly. Working in batches, purée soup in blender until smooth. Pour soup into saucepan. Stir in cream and bleu cheese. Simmer over medium heat until cheese melts and soup is smooth, whisking constantly, about 2 minutes. Season to taste with salt and pepper. Ladle into bowls. Sprinkle with chives and serve. Makes 6 servings.

COLD ROASTED CORN SOUP WITH DUNGENESS CRAB

6 ears of fresh corn, roasted, shucked
2 cups cold whole milk
½ teaspoon salt
¾ teaspoon black pepper
2 tablespoons chopped fresh chives
8 ounces dungeness crab
4 teaspoons Asian red chili oil

Cook corn on open flame of grill or wood fire (I like to use Alderwood). When cool enough to handle, shuck and cut off kernels and scrape cobs over a bowl to extract juice, then purée in batches in a blender with milk, salt, and pepper. Force purée through a very fine sieve into a bowl, discard solids, and stir in chives. Cut crab shell and extract meat, then cut into 1/4" pieces. Serve soup drizzled with chili oil and sprinkled with crab meat. Serves 4.

TOASTED ALMOND CHILLED SOUP

5 slices white bread
3 cups cold water
1 cup toasted almonds
2 garlic cloves, sliced
5 tablespoons extra virgin olive oil
1 ½ tablespoon sherry
salt and freshly ground white pepper

Toasted sliced almonds
Kiwi slices

Break the bread into a large bowl and pour 2/3 cup of the water on top. Leave to stand for five minutes. Place the almonds and garlic in a food processor and process until finely ground. Blend in the soaked bread. Gradually add the oil until the mixture forms a smooth paste. Add the sherry and remaining cold water and process until smooth. Transfer to a bowl and season with salt and pepper, adding a little more water if the soup is too thick. Chill for at least 3 hours. Serve with toasted almonds and sliced kiwi on top. Serves 6.

WHOLE WHEAT GARLIC CROUTONS ON CARROT SOUP

1 tablespoon olive oil
1 large onion, chopped
3 3/4 cups sliced carrots
1 teaspoon each ground coriander, ground cumin, and cayenne pepper
3 3/4 cups vegetable stock
salt and freshly ground pepper
sprigs of fresh cilantro to garnish

extra virgin olive oil
2 garlic cloves, crushed
4 slices whole wheat bread, crusts removed, cut into 1/2″ cubes

To make the soup, heat the oil in a large saucepan. Add the onion and carrots and cook slowly for 5 minutes, stirring occasionally. Add the ground spices and cook for 1 minute longer, stirring. Stir in the stock and bring to a boil. Cover and simmer for about 45 minutes until the carrots are tender. Meanwhile, make the garlic croutons. Heat the oil in a skillet add the garlic and cook slowly for 30 seconds. Add the bread cubes, turn them over in the oil and fry over medium heat for a few minutes until crisp and golden brown all over, turning frequently. Drain on paper towels and keep warm. Purée the soup in a food processor until smooth. Season to taste with salt and pepper. Return the soup to the saucepan and reheat slowly. Serve hot, sprinkled with whole wheat garlic croutons and garnished with cilantro. Serves 6.

RED SOUP

1 tablespoon extra virgin olive oil
2 1/2 cups sliced red onions
2 garlic cloves, crushed
2 1/2 cups cooked beets, julienned
1 1/4 quart vegetable stock
1 cup cooked barley
2 tablespoons a raspberry vinegar
salt and freshly ground black pepper
fromage blanc and chives for garnish

Heat the olive oil in a large saucepan. Add the onions and garlic. Cook slowly for about 20 minutes, or until soft and tender, stirring occasionally. Add the beets, stock, barley, and vinegar and heat through. Season and garnish with fromage blanc and chives. Serves 6.

RISOTTO SOUP

1 ½ pounds fresh spinach, washed
3 tablespoons extra virgin olive oil
1 small white onion, minced
2 garlic cloves, minced
1 small fresh red chili, seeded and minced
½ cup risotto rice
1 ¼ quart vegetable stock
salt and freshly ground black pepper
4 tablespoons grated Asiago cheese, to serve

Place the spinach in a large pan with just the water that clings to its leaves after washing. Add a large salt and heat gently until the spinach wilts. Remove from the heat and drain, reserving any liquid. Chop the spinach using a food processor and purée coarsely. Heat the oil in a large saucepan. Add the onion, garlic, and chili and cook for 4 to 5 minutes until soft. Stir in the rice until well coated. Pour in the stock and reserved spinach liquid. Bring to a boil. Lower the heat and simmer for 10 minutes. Add the spinach and cook for 5 to 7 minutes longer, until the rice is tender. Season with salt and freshly ground pepper. Serve with the Asiago cheese. Serves 4.

BASATO SOUP

1 tablespoon extra virgin olive oil
2 tablespoons unsalted butter
1 medium Vidalia onion, minced
2 pounds ripe plum tomatoes, roughly chopped
1 garlic clove, roughly chopped
3 cups vegetable stock
½ cup dry white wine
2 tablespoons sun-dried tomatoes, pureed into paste
2 tablespoons shredded fresh basil, plus a few whole leaves to garnish
2/3 cup heavy cream, 40%
salt and freshly ground black pepper

Heat the oil and butter in a large saucepan until foaming. Add the onion and cook slowly for about 5 minutes, stirring frequently, until soft, but do not let brown. Stir in the tomatoes and garlic, stock, white wine, and sun-dried tomato paste, with salt and pepper to taste. Bring to a boil. Lower the heat, cover the pan, and simmer slowly for 20 minutes, stirring occasionally to stop the tomatoes from sticking to the bottom. Process the soup with the shredded basil in a food processor. Press through a strainer into sauce pan. Add the heavy cream and heat through, stirring: do not let the soup approach the boiling point. Check the consistency and add more stock, if necessary. Adjust the seasoning to taste and garnish with whole basil leaves. Serves 6.

CHILLED SOUP
WITH AVOCADO AND GINGER

2 tablespoons unsalted butter
3 large shallots, minced
1 tablespoon minced peel fresh ginger
30 ounces chicken stock
2 tablespoons fresh squeezed lime juice
1 ¼ teaspoon cayenne pepper
2 large ripe avocados, halved, pitted, peeled and mashed
½ cup heavy cream, 40%
Cilantro and lime slices for garnish

Melt butter in saucepan over medium heat. Add minced shallots and minced ginger and sauté 1 minute. Add chicken stock, lime juice and cayenne pepper; bring to boil. Reduce heat to medium low and simmer 3 minutes. Transfer mixture to large bowl. Puree avocados and cream in food processor. Whisk into soup. Season with salt and pepper. Refrigerate until cold: serves 6.

VEGETABLE STOCK

2 leeks, roughly chopped
3 celery stalks, roughly chopped
1 large onion, with skin, chopped
2 pieces fresh ginger root, chopped
1 yellow bell pepper, seeded and chopped
1 parsnip, chopped
mushroom stalks
tomato peelings
3 tablespoons light soy sauce
3 bay leaves
a bunch of parsley stems
3 sprigs of fresh thyme
1 sprig of fresh rosemary
2 teaspoons salt
freshly ground black pepper
3 3/4 quarts cold water

Put all the ingredients into a very large saucepan. Bring slowly to a boil. Lower the heat and simmer for 30 minutes, stirring from time to time. Leave to cool. Strain, then discard the vegetables: the stock is ready to use. Alternatively, chill or freeze the stock and keep it to use as required. Makes 2 ¾ quarts.

CHICKEN STOCK

2 ½ to 3 pounds chicken or turkey, (wings, backs and necks)
2 large onions, unpeeled, quartered (any onion will do)
1 tablespoon extra virgin olive oil
4 ¼ quarts cold water
2 carrots, roughly chopped
2 celery stalks, with leaves, roughly chopped
small handful of fresh parsley
a few sprigs of fresh thyme, or 3/4 teaspoon dried thyme
2 bay leaves
10 black peppercorns, crushed

Combine the poultry wings, backs, and necks in a stock pot with the onion quarters and the oil. Cook over medium heat, stirring occasionally, until the poultry and onions are lightly and evenly brown. Add the water and stir well to mix in the sediment on the bottom of the pan. Bring to a boil and skim off the impurities as they will rise to the surface of the stock. Add the chopped carrots and celery, fresh parsley, thyme, bay leaves, and black peppercorns. Lower the heat, partly cover the stock pot and simmer the stock for about 3 hours. Strain the stock through a strainer into a bowl and lead to cool. Chill in refrigerator for an hour. When cold, carefully remove the layer of fat that will have set on the surface. Store in the refrigerator for three to four days, or freeze until required. Makes 2 ¾ quarts.

BEEF STOCK

4 pounds beef bones, such as leg, and shank, cut into 2 1/2 inch pieces
2 large onions, unpeeled and quartered
2 large carrots, roughly chopped
2 celery stalks, with leaves, roughly chopped
2 large tomatoes, coarsely chopped
5 quarts cold water
a handful of parsley stems
few sprigs of fresh thyme or 3/4 teaspoon dried thyme
2 bay leaves
10 black peppercorns, crushed

Preheat the oven to 450°. Place the bones in a roasting pan and roast, turning them occasionally, for 30 minutes until they start to brown. Add the onions, carrots, celery, and tomatoes and baste with the fat in the pan. Roast for 20 to 30 minutes longer until the bones are very brown. Stir and baste occasionally. Transfer the bones and roasted vegetables to a stock pot. Spoon off the fat from the roasting pan. Add a little of the water to the roasting pan and bring to a boil on the stovetop, stirring well to scrape up any browned bits. Pour this liquid into the stock pot. Add the remaining water to the pot. Bring just to a boil, skimming frequently to remove all the foam from the surface. Add the parsley, thyme, bay leaves, and peppercorns. Lower the heat, partly cover the pot, and simmer the stock for 4 to 6 hours. The bones and vegetables should always be covered with liquid, top with a little boiling water from time to time if necessary. Strain the stock through a colander. Skim as much fat as possible from the surface. If possible, cool the stock and then refrigerate it: the fat will rise to the top and set in a layer that can be removed easily. Makes 2 ¼ quarts.

PASTA

GNOCCHI WITH CAULIFLOWER

1 medium cauliflower

2 cups whole milk

1 bay leaf

1/4 cup unsalted butter

1/2 cup flour

salt and freshly ground black pepper

3/4 cup freshly grated Parmesan cheese

1 1/4 pound gnocchi, cooked as described on package

Bring a steamer pot to boil and steam cauliflower about 8-10 minutes, or until just tender. Remove from steamer to cool. Chop the cauliflower into bite size pieces and set aside. Do not discard the steamer water. Make a bechamel sauce by gently heating the milk with the bay leaf in a small saucepan, do not let it boil. Melt the butter in a medium heavy saucepan. Add the flour, and mix it in well with a wire whisk, ensuring there are no lumps. Cook for 2 to 3 minutes, but do not let the butter burn. Strain the hot milk into the flour and butter mixture all at once, and mix smoothly with a whisk. Bring the sauce to the boil, stirring constantly, and cook for 4 to 5 minutes more. Season with salt and pepper. Add the cheese, and stir over low heat until it melts. Stir in the cauliflower. Bring the steamer water back to the boil. Add salt, and stir in the gnocchi. Cook until tender. Drain, place the pasta into a warm serving bowl. Pour over the sauce. Mix well, and serve. Serves 6.

FARFALLE WITH SHRIMP

3 tablespoons extra virgin olive oil
2 tablespoons unsalted butter
2 spring onions, chopped
12 ounces fresh, peeled and deveined shrimp
1 ¼ cups fresh peas
1 ¼ pounds of farfalle
1 cup dry white wine
1/8 teaspoon saffron
salt and freshly ground black pepper
2 tablespoons lemon zest
2 tablespoons chopped fresh dill

Bring a large pan of water to boil. Heat the oil and butter in a large frying pan and sauté the spring onions lightly. Add the shrimp and peas, and cook for 2 to 3 minutes. Add salt and the pasta to the boiling water. Stir the wine and saffron into the shrimp mixture. Raise the heat and cook until the wine is reduced by about half. Add salt and pepper to taste. Cover the pan and reduce the heat to low. Drain the pasta when it is al dente. Add it to the pan with the sauce. Stir over high heat for 2 to 3 minutes, coating the pasta with the sauce. Sprinkle with the fresh dill and lemon zest. Serves 4.

TAGLIETELLI
WITH CLAMS AND SAUSAGE

2 tablespoons extra virgin olive oil
¼ pound andouille sausage, cut into 1/2″ slices
¼ cup chopped onions
3 cloves garlic, chopped
36 Little neck clams, scrubbed
1 cup chopped fresh plum tomatoes
½ cup dry white wine
1 pound taglietelli
1 tablespoon chopped fresh Italian parsley
1 tablespoon finely shredded fresh basil

Heat the oil in a heavy pot. Add the sausage, onions and garlic. Sauté over low heat until the onions are tender. Stir in the clams, tomatoes and wine, cover the pot and cook over medium low heat until the clams open. Cook the pasta in a large pot until just tender. Drain. Serve the clams in their shells along with the sauce over the taglietelli. Sprinkle with parsley and basil. Serves 6.

FETTUCCINI WITH LEMON CHICKEN AND PINENUTS

2 tablespoons, plus 2/3 cup extra virgin olive oil
¾ pound boneless, skinless chicken breast

12 ounces fettuccini
2 ½ cups snow peas, cut in matchstick strips
¾ cup toasted pine nuts
¾ cup chopped fresh Italian parsley
3 tablespoons fresh squeezed lemon juice
2 tablespoons white sugar
2 ½ tablespoons stoneground mustard

Heat 1 tablespoon of oil in large nonstick skillet over medium heat. Add chicken and sauté until cooked through, about 5 minutes per side. Cool. Julienne chicken in ¼ inch thick strips. Cook pasta in large pot of boiling salted water until tender. Drain well; transfer to large bowl. Add 1 tablespoon oil; toss to coat. Add chicken, snow peas, pine nuts and parsley; toss to incorporate all ingredients. Whisk lemon juice, sugar and mustard in small bowl. Add remaining. ¾ cup oil in thin stream, whisking constantly. Season to taste with salt and pepper. Toss pasta with enough dressing to coat. Serves 6.

CELOPHANE NOODLES AND PORK

½ cup chicken stock
¼ cup plus 2 tablespoons light soy sauce
1 tablespoon stoneground mustard
1 tablespoon unseasoned rice vinegar
1 teaspoon Asian sesame oil
½ teaspoon chili oil
1 medium carrot, fine julienne
1 pound celophane noodles
2 tablespoons vegetable oil
¾ pound boneless pork, preferably shoulder thinly sliced across the grain
salt and freshly ground pepper
3 tablespoons finely slivered fresh ginger
1 small green bell pepper, fine julienne
2 scallions, cut fine julienne
1 cup broco bean sprouts

In a small bowl, combine the stock, soy sauce, mustard, vinegar, sesame oil and chili oil. In a large pot of boiling water, blanch the carrot for 1 minute. Using a slotted spoon, transfer the carrot to a plate. Add the noodles to the pot and cook, stirring, until they are al dente, about 5 minutes. Drain the noodles and return them to the pot. Fill the pot with cold water and swish the noodles to cool them. Drain and repeat. Transfer to cool the noodles to a colander and lift them occasionally with your fingers to help dry them out. Meanwhile, in a large, deep skillet, heat the vegetable oil until shimmering. Add the pork slices in a single layer, season with salt and pepper and cook over high heat, without stirring, until browned on the bottom, about 2 minutes. Stir a few times, then add the ginger and stir fry over moderately high heat until fragrant, about 2 minutes. Add the bell pepper and carrot and stir fry for 1 minute. Add the noodles to the skillet and toss until well combined. Add the soy sauce mixture, scallions and bean sprouts and toss until heated through. Transfer to a large shallow bowl and serve. Serves 6.

MAPLE ROASTED BUTTERNUT SQUASH, PROSCIUTTO AND RIGATONI

1, 1 ¾ pound butternut squash, peeled and cut into 1/2″ dice, 2 cups
¼ cup extra virgin olive oil
½ cup maple syrup
salt and freshly ground black pepper
¾ pound rigatoni pasta
3 ounces thickly sliced prosciutto, cut into 1/4″ dice
2 shallots, thinly sliced
12 sage leaves, coarse chopped
¼ teaspoon crushed red pepper
½ cup freshly grated pecorino romano cheese

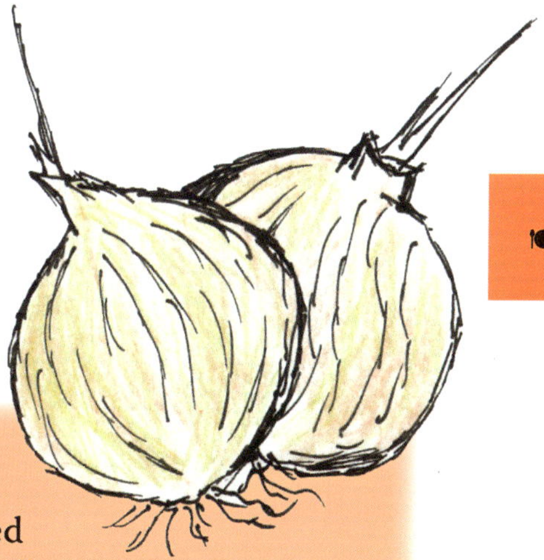

Preheat the oven to 425°. On a medium, rimmed baking sheet, toss the squash with 1 tablespoon of the olive oil and syrup. Roast for 15 minutes, tossing once, until browned and tender; season with salt. Meanwhile, in a pot of boiling salted water, cook the rigatoni until just al dente. Drain, reserving 1 cup of the cooking water. Heat the remaining 3 tablespoons of olive oil in a large skillet. Add the prosciutto and cook over moderate heat until lightly browned, about 5 minutes. Add the shallots, sage, crushed red pepper and a generous pinch of black pepper and cook until the shallots are soft, about 4 minutes. Add the squash, rigatoni and reserved cooking water and cook over moderate heat, tossing gently, until the sauce is thickened and the pasta is al dente, 2 to 3 minutes; season with salt. Stir in the ½ cup of pecorino cheese. Serves 4.

ORZO WITH LAMB

1 cup orzo

3 tablespoons stoneground mustard

1 ½ tablespoons boiling water

1 ½ tablespoons lemon juice

2 cloves garlic, minced

½ cup olive oil

1 tablespoon heavy cream, 40%

salt and freshly ground pepper

¾ pound cooked, preferably rare, lamb, cut julienned

½ pound green beans, blanched and cut into julienned strips

1 mall red onion, sliced into thin rings

1 small red bell pepper, thinly sliced

¼ cup minced fresh parsley

In a large saucepan of boiling water, cook the orzo for 6 to 8 minutes, or until just tender. Drain. In a large salad bowl combine the mustard, boiling water, lemon juice and garlic. Add the olive oil in a stream, whisking until well combined, then whisk in the heavy cream. Add salt and pepper to taste. Stir in the orzo, lamb, green beans, onions, bell peppers and parsley. Chill for at least one hour, tossing occasionally. Serves 4.

FRUITI DE MAR LASAGNA

8 whole tomatoes
½ cup diced onion
2 cloves garlic, minced
3 tablespoons olive oil, divided
1 ½ pounds haddock, or pollack fillets
salt and freshly ground pepper
6 ounces tomato paste
1 pound shrimp, peeled and deveined
1 pound lobster meat
3 eggs
1 pound ricotta cheese
2 tablespoons grated Parmesan cheese
1 pound of lasagna, cooked al dente
1 ½ cups shredded provolone cheese, divided

Blend the tomatoes in a food processor. In a large saucepan, sauté the onions and garlic in 2 tablespoons of the oil. Add the fish and salt and pepper to taste. Cover the pan and simmer, stirring occasionally, until the fish flakes easily, about 10 minutes. Add the tomatoes, bring to a boil, lower the heat, cover and simmer for 5 minutes. Add the tomato paste and simmer, uncovered, for 10 minutes, stirring occasionally. Meanwhile, in a medium skillet, heat the remaining 1 tablespoon oil. Add the shrimp and lobster, cook lightly until the shrimp curl and the lobster is pink. Strain and add to the fish sauce. If the shrimp are large, cut them into bite size pieces, or slice in half before adding. Beat the eggs in a medium bowl, add the ricotta and Parmesan cheeses and season with salt and pepper to taste. Mix well. Pour about one quarter of the fish sauce into a 15" x 11" lasagna pan and cover with one third of the lasagna. Dot with about one third of the cheese mixture and sprinkle with one third of the provolone. Continue to layer the fish sauce, lasagna and cheeses until you have three layers of each. Top with the remaining sauce, cover with foil and bake in a preheated 350° oven for 30 minutes. Serves 10.

GREEN TOMATO SAUCE AND CAVATELLI

1 tablespoon extra virgin olive oil
1 medium onion, finely chopped
1 teaspoon finely chopped garlic
3 large green tomatoes, thinly sliced, about 4 cups
¼ cup chicken stock
2 tablespoon coarsely chopped fresh basil
1 tablespoon finely chopped fresh parsley
salt and freshly ground pepper
8 ounces of cavatelli pasta
3 tablespoons grated Parmesan cheese
chopped fresh parsley

Heat the oil in a large saucepan. Add the onions and sauté over medium heat until they begin to turn golden. Add the garlic and cook for about one minute, then add the tomatoes and simmer, stirring occasionally, for 5 minutes. Add ¼ cup of the stock and the basil, parsley and salt and pepper to taste. Cover and simmer for 20 minutes, adding more stock if necessary. When the sauce is nearly done, cook the pasta until just tender. Drain well and toss with the sauce. Add the cheese, mix and serve, garnish with chopped parsley. Serves 4.

BAY SCALLOP STEW

1 cup chopped red onion
6 cloves garlic, minced
1 tablespoon extra virgin olive oil
2 pounds fresh tomatoes, cooked down
4 tablespoons fresh parsley
4 tablespoons fresh basil
¼ teaspoon red pepper flakes
2 pound bay scallops
9 ounces cheese tortellini
3 tablespoons lemon zest

In a soup pot, cook the onions and garlic in the oil until tender. Stir in the tomatoes, parsley, basil and red pepper flakes. Bring to a boil, add the scallops, and reduce the heat and simmer for 3 to 5 minutes. Be sure to cook the stew gently after you add the scallops so they don't toughen. Cook tortellini just al dente, spoon into bowls and ladle stew over. Sprinkle with lemon zest. Serves 6.

LEEK TARRAGON CREAM SAUCE OVER LOBSTER

1 stick unsalted butter
4 large leeks, white and tender green parts, thinly sliced crosswise
¼ cup white wine, Riesling works well
1 tablespoon finely chopped tarragon, plus one quarter cup leaves
1 cup heavy cream, 40%
salt and freshly ground black pepper
1 carrot, shredded
1 teaspoon fresh squeezed lemon juice
2 tablespoons water
2 pound cooked a lobster meat
1 pound cappellini pasta

In a large saucepan, melt 3 tablespoons of the butter. Add the leeks and cook over moderate heat, stirring occasionally, until just tender, about 5 minutes. Add the wine and chopped tarragon and cook until the wine evaporates, 2 to 3 minutes. Add the cream and season with salt and pepper. Cover partially and cook over low heat until the cream is slightly reduced, about 10 minutes. Scrape the mixture into a blender and purée until smooth. Return the creamy leek sauce to the saucepan and season with salt and pepper. Cover and keep warm. Melt 1 tablespoon of the butter in a small skillet. Add the shredded beet, season with salt and pepper and cook over moderately high heat, stirring constantly, until tender, about 8 minutes. Stir in the lemon juice. In a medium saucepan, melt the remaining 4 tablespoons of butter in the water over moderately low heat, whisking constantly. Add the lobster meat and cook just until heated through, 1 to 2 minutes. Keep warm. Meanwhile, cook the pasta in a large pot of boiling salted water until barely al dente. Drain, reserving 1 cup of the pasta cooking water. Return the pasta to the pot and add the leek sauce, reserved pasta water and the butter from the lobster; season with salt and pepper and toss to coat. Transfer the pasta to plates and top with the lobster meat. Garnish with the carrots and tarragon leaves and serve at once. Serves 6.

JAMBALAYA PENNE

4 tablespoons extra virgin olive oil
1 pound andouille sausage, then thinly sliced crosswise
1 medium white onion, chopped
1 large green bell pepper, chopped
5 green onion, thinly sliced
1 celery stalk, chopped
5 garlic cloves, chopped
2 bay leaves
2 tablespoons fresh chopped oregano
¾ teaspoon ground cumin
¼ teaspoon cayenne pepper
¼ teaspoon ground allspice
1 28 ounce can crushed tomatoes with added puree
1 pound diced roma tomatoes, reserve any juice
1 teaspoon Worcestershire sauce
½ teaspoon hot pepper sauce
1 pound penne pasta
11/2 pounds uncooked large shrimp, peeled, deveined
Freshly grated parmesan cheese

Heat 2 tablespoons oil in heavy pot over medium heat. Add sausages; sauté until light brown, about 5 minutes. Using slotted spoon, transfer sausages to paper towels. Pour drippings from pot; discard. Add remaining 2 tablespoons oil to pot and heat over medium heat. Stir in onion and next 9 ingredients. Cover and cook until vegetables are almost tender, stirring often, about 8 minutes. Stir in crushed tomatoes and diced tomatoes with juices and bring to boil. Reduce heat, cover and simmer 15 minutes to blend flavors. Stir in sausages, Worcestershire sauce and hot pepper sauce; simmer uncovered until sauce thickens slightly, about 5 minutes longer. Season to taste with salt and pepper. Discard bay leaves. Meanwhile, cook pasta in large pot of boiling salted water until just tender but still firm to bite. Remove from heat. Add shrimp to pot; cover and let stand just until shrimp are pink on outside and opaque in center, about 2 minutes. Drain pasta and shrimp; return to pot. Add sauce and toss to blend. Transfer to bowl. Top with parmesan cheese. Serves 6.

ENTRÉES

ROAST OF VENISON

1 venison roast, 3 to 4 pounds
12 whole garlic cloves, peeled
2 tablespoons fresh rosemary, crushed
1 1/2 teaspoons onion powder, divided
1 teaspoon garlic powder
1 tablespoon fresh thyme
7 medium carrots, quartered
5 small onions, quartered
2 cups beef stock
2 tablespoons cornstarch
3 tablespoons cold water
Maple syrup

Cut deep slits in roast; place the garlic clove in each slit. Pierce roast in several places with a meat fork. Combine rosemary, 1 teaspoon onion powder, garlic powder and thyme; rub over an entire roast. Cover; refrigerate for two hours. Add 1/2" of water to a roasting pan. Place the roast, carrots and onions in pan. Cover and bake at 325° for 2 ½ to 3 hours or until meat thermometer reads 160°. Remove meat and vegetables to a serving platter; keep warm, strain drippings into a measuring cup. In a sauce pan, combine 3 cups drippings, stock, and remaining onion powder. Combine cornstarch and cold water until smooth; stir into drippings, add maple syrup to taste. Bring to a boil; cook and stir for 2 minutes or until thickened. Serve with roast. Serves 8.

CURRIED RED SNAPPER

1 ½ pounds fresh red snapper
2 medium red onions, chopped
2 celery ribs, chopped
1 tablespoon unsalted butter
½ teaspoon ground coriander
½ teaspoon ground cumin
1 ½ inch piece ginger, shredded
¾ teaspoons salt
¼ cup coconut milk

Place the fish in a greased 13" x 9" by 2 inch baking dish. In a skillet, sauté the onions, ginger and celery in butter until tender. Add coriander, cumin and salt; mix well. Remove from the heat; stir in coconut milk. Spoon over fish. Bake, uncovered, at 350° for 25 minutes or until fish flakes easily with a fork. Serves 6.

SCALLOPS, PROSCIUTTO AND ASPARAGUS

1 pound asparagus
3 1/2 tablespoons unsalted butter
1 ounce a thinly sliced prosciutto, cut into 1/2" wide strips
1 pound sea scallops
salt and freshly ground black pepper
1/2 teaspoon finely grated lemon zest
2 tablespoons fresh lemon juice
1/4 cup chicken stock

Cook the asparagus and a large saucepan over boiling salted water until tender, about 8 minutes. Using tongs, transfer the asparagus to a colander and leave the pan of water simmering on the stove. Melt 1 tablespoon of the butter in a large skillet. Add the prosciutto and cook over low heat until crisp, about 4 minutes. Transfer the prosciutto to a plate. Melt 2 tablespoons of the butter in a skillet. Add the scallops, season with salt and pepper and cook over moderately high heat until brown, about 2 minutes per side. Transfer the scallops to a plate. Add the lemon zest to the skillet and cook over moderate heat until browned, about 1 minute. Add the lemon juice and simmer for 10 seconds. Add the stock and simmer, scraping the bottom of the skillet, until reduced to a rich glaze, about 3 minutes. Swirl in the remaining ½ tablespoon of butter. Return the scallops, along with any juices, to the skillet and cook over low heat until heated through. Return the asparagus to the simmering water to heat through. Season the sauce with salt and pepper. Using tongs transfer the asparagus to a large platter and spoon the scallops and sauce over it. Topped with fried prosciutto and serve. Serves 4.

PORK LOIN SAUERBRATEN

2 teaspoons salt
1 teaspoon ground ginger
1 pork loin roast, bone in, about 4 pounds
2 ½ cups water
2 cups cider vinegar
2 medium onions, sliced
1/3 cup white granulated sugar
2 tablespoons mixed pickling spices
1 teaspoon whole peppercorns
8 whole cloves
2 bay leaves
2 tablespoons of vegetable oil
16 gingersnaps, crushed

Combine salt and ginger; rub over roast. Place in a deep glass bowl. In a saucepan, combine water, vinegar, onions, sugar, pickling spices, peppercorns, cloves and bay leaves; bring to a boil. Pour over roast; turn to coat. Cover and refrigerate for 2 days, turning twice a day. Remove roast, reserving marinade; Pat roast dry. In a large kettle or Dutch oven, brown roast on all sides in oil. Strain marinade, reserving half of the onions and seasonings. Pour 1 cup of marinade and reserved onions and seasonings over roast, cover and refrigerate remaining marinade. Bring to a boil. Reduce heat; cover and simmer for3 hours or until meat is tender. Strain cooking liquid, discarding the onions and seasonings. Measure liquid; if necessary, add enough to reserved marinade to equal 3 cups. Pour into a saucepan; bring to a rolling boil. Add gingersnaps; simmer until gravy is thickened. Serves 14.

PECAN TROUT WITH ARTICHOKE TARTER SAUCE

Trout:
¼ cup whole milk
1 extra large egg
1 cup pecan pieces, toasted
1 ½ cups fresh bread crumbs made from French bread, or panko
4- 12 ounces trout, butterflied
½ cup all-purpose flour
8 tablespoons extra virgin olive oil

Artichoke tartar sauce:
1- 13 ¾ ounce can artichoke bottoms, drained, diced
¾ cup mayonnaise
1/3 cup finely chopped red onion
¼ cup minced green onion
2 tablespoons drained capers
2 tablespoons finely cornichons
1 tablespoon chopped fresh parsley

For the tartar sauce:

Stir all ingredients in medium bowl to combine. Cover and chill at least 30 minutes. (Can be made up to two days ahead. Keep chilled.)

For the Trout:

Preheat oven to 300°. Whisk milk and egg in small bowl to blend. Combine pecans and breadcrumbs or Panko in processor; blend until finely ground. Open trout fillets, skin side down. Sprinkle flesh with salt and freshly ground pepper, then with flour, shaking off excess. Brush floured side with egg mixture, then cover with pecan mixture, pressing to adhere. Repeat with remaining trout, heat 2 tablespoons oil in each of two large skillets over medium-high heat. Place one trout, pecan side down, in each skillet and sauté until golden brown, about 3 minutes. Turn and cook another 2 minutes. Repeat. Serves 4.

MEATLOAF WITH MUSTARD DILL SAUCE

6 tablespoons sour cream
2 ½ tablespoons chopped fresh dill
4 teaspoons stoneground mustard
5 ounces lean ground beef
5 ounces ground pork
5 ounces ground veal
2/3 cup fresh breadcrumbs made from whole wheat bread
1/3 cup chopped onion
¼ teaspoon ground allspice

Preheat oven to 450°. Stir 4 tablespoons sour cream, 1 tablespoon dill and 1 teaspoon mustard in small bowl for sauce. Combine beef, pork, veal and breadcrumbs, onion and allspice in large bowl. Add remaining 2 tablespoons sour cream, 1 1/2 tablespoon dill and 3 teaspoons mustard and blend well. Shape mixture into 2 loaf pans. Place loaves on baking sheet. Bake until cooked through about 35 minutes. Serve meat loaves with sauce. Serves 4.

FRIED RICE WITH SHIITAKE MUSHROOMS AND WILTED CABBAGE

1½ cups water
½ teaspoon salt
¾ cup natural black rice
2 ½ tablespoons vegetable oil
2 extra large eggs, beaten
8 ounces fresh shiitake mushrooms, stems removed, sliced
1 green pepper julienned
2 teaspoons minced peeled fresh ginger
2 cups shredded napa cabbage
2 green onions, chopped
1 tablespoon soy sauce

Bring 1½ cups water and salt to boil in medium saucepan over high heat. Mix in rice. Reduce heat to low, cover and cook until rice is tender and water is absorbed, about 40 minutes. Observe directions on package. Meanwhile, heat 1 tablespoon oil in medium nonstick skillet over medium heat. Add eggs. Cook without stirring until eggs are set and bottom is brown, lifting edge of eggs occasionally to let onion cooked portion runs underneath, about 3 minutes. Turn out egg pancake. Cut in half and cut crosswise into thin strips. Heat 1½ tablespoons oil in same skillet over medium-high heat. Add mushrooms; sauté 4 minutes. Add pepper, cabbage and ginger; sauté 3 minutes. Add rice, egg strips, onions and 1 tablespoon soy sauce; toss. Season with salt and freshly ground pepper. Serves 2.

GARLIC PORK TENDERLOIN WITH PRUNES

8 ounces, 1 1/3 cups, pitted prunes
1 1/3 cups water
2/3 cup sherry wine vinegar
½ cup white granulated sugar
¼ cup extra virgin olive oil
6 garlic cloves
2 tablespoons chopped fresh rosemary
2 teaspoons cracked black pepper
1½ pounds pork tenderloins
crushed red pepper
12 cups sliced escarole, about 1 large head
1 cup chicken stock

Bring pitted prunes, 1 1/3 cups water, the sherry wine vinegar and white sugar to boil in heavy medium saucepan, stirring until sugar dissolves. Reduce heat to medium and cook until liquid is syrupy, about 20 minutes. Set prunes a side. Preheat oven to 400°. Blend 1/4 cup olive oil, garlic cloves, chopped fresh rosemary and cracked black pepper and food processor to form paste. Place pork tenderloins in roasting pan; rub with 3 1/2 tablespoons garlic paste. Set remaining garlic paste aside. Roast pork tenderloins until thermometer inserted into thickest part registers 150 degrees, about 30 minutes. Meanwhile heat remaining garlic paste and dried crushed red pepper in large heavy saucepan over medium-high heat. Add 12 cups sliced escarole; cover and cook until wilted, about 6 minutes. Mix in chicken stock. Transfer pork to work surface and slice. Mix any pan juices from pork into prunes and bring to simmer. Divide escarole among 6 plates. Top with pork, then prunes. Serves 6.

MEDITERRANEAN LAMB

1 large onion, chopped
2 tablespoons extra virgin olive oil
1 boneless lamb shoulder roast, 2 1/2 to 3 pounds, cubed
1 teaspoon ground cumin
1 teaspoon ground cinnamon
1 teaspoon ground coriander
salt and fresh ground pepper to taste
½ cup dried apricots, halved
¼ cup orange juice
1tablespoon ground almonds
½ teaspoon orange zest
1 ¼ cups chicken stock
1 tablespoon toasted sesame seeds

In a large skillet, sauté onion in oil until tender. Add the lamb, cumin, cinnamon, coriander, salt and fresh ground pepper. Cook and stir for 5 minutes or until meat is browned. Add apricots, orange juice, almonds and orange zest. Transfer to a baking dish. Stir in stock. Cover and bake at 350° for 1 ½ hours or until meat is tender. Sprinkle with sesame seeds. Serves 8.

PORTOBELLO BURGERS

1/3 cup balsamic vinaigrette
1 tablespoon chopped fresh rosemary
2 round ciabatta rolls, split
2 large portobello mushrooms, about 5 inches in diameter, stemmed
4 slices mozzarella cheese
1 beefsteak tomato, thinly sliced
1 cup, loosely packed, arugula leaves

Prepare BBQ, medium-high heat. Whisk vinaigrette and rosemary in small bowl. Brush cut sides of rolls with vinaigrette. Place rolls on grill, cut side down. Grilled until lightly toasted, about one minute. Brush mushrooms on both sides with vinaigrette. Sprinkle generously with salt and freshly ground black pepper. Place mushrooms on grill, dark gills side down. Close grill or cover mushrooms with small metal roasting pan; cook until mushrooms begin to soften, brushing with vinaigrette once, about 5 minutes. Turn mushrooms over. Cover; grill until tender when pierced with a knife, about 7 minutes longer. Place 2 cheese slices on each mushroom. Cover; grill until cheese melts, about 1 minute. Place one mushroom on bottom half of each roll. Top each with tomato, arugula and top half of the roll. Serves 2.

LEMON AND GARLIC GRILLED LOBSTER

1 ½ cups extra virgin olive oil
9 tablespoons soy sauce
¼ cup fresh squeezed lemon juice
6 garlic cloves, minced
6 tablespoons minced peeled fresh ginger
6, 2 pound live lobsters
6 tablespoons chopped green onions

Cook first 5 ingredients in medium saucepan over low heat until garlic and ginger begin to brown, about 8 minutes. Set aside. Prepare barbecue, medium-high heat. Drop one lobster headfirst into large pot of boiling water. Cover; cook 3 minutes, lobster will not be fully cooked. Using tongs, transfer lobster to baking sheet. Return water to boil. Repeat with remaining lobsters. Transfer one lobster, shelled side down, to work surface. Place tip of large knife in center of lobster. Cut lobster lengthwise in half from center to end of head, knife might not cut through shell, then cut in half from center to end of tail. Use poultry shears to cut through shell if necessary. Repeat with remaining lobsters. Place lobster halves, meat side up, on barbecue. Brush meat with some basting sauce; sprinkle with salt and pepper. Cover barbecue; grill lobsters until just opaque in thickest portion of tale, about 9 minutes. Remove from barbecue; arrange lobsters on platter. Brush with more sauce and sprinkle with green onions.

Serves 6.

SOLE WITH OYSTER MUSHROOMS AND ASPARAGUS TIPS

24 thin asparagus spears
8 tablespoons, one stick, unsalted butter
12 ounces fresh oyster mushrooms, sliced
¾ cup chopped seeded peeled tomatoes, about 2 large
1 ½ tablespoons fresh squeezed lemon juice
2 whole pompano, split and butterflied
2 tablespoons chopped fresh at Italian parsley

Cut 2 inch-long tips from asparagus spears, reserve remaining asparagus pieces for another use. Cook asparagus tips in saucepan of boiling salted water until crisp tender, about 3 minutes. Drain. Place asparagus tips in bowl filled with ice water to cool. Drain. Set aside. Melt 3 tablespoons butter in large nonstick skillet over medium heat. Add mushrooms, cover and cook until tender, stirring occasionally, about 10 minutes. Add asparagus tips,3 tablespoons butter and tomatoes; stir until butter melts and vegetables are heated through, about 1 minute. Stir in lemon juice. Season to taste with salt and pepper. Melt remaining 2 tablespoons butter in another large nonstick skillet over medium-high heat. Sprinkle fish with salt and freshly ground pepper. Add a fish fillets to skillet and cook until just opaque in center, about 2 minutes per side. Place to fish fillets in center of each of 4 plates. Top with mushroom mixture, sprinkle with parsley. Serves 4.

GORGONZOLA CHEESE AND HERB SOUFFLE

7 tablespoons grated Parmesan cheese
3/4 cup whole milk
3 large egg yolks
2 1/2 tablespoons butter
1/2 cup chopped red onion
1 teaspoon chopped fresh thyme
1/2 teaspoon chopped fresh rosemary
2 tablespoons all-purpose flour
1 cup crumbled gorgonzola cheese
3/4 teaspoons salt
1/4 teaspoon fresh ground white pepper
large pinch of cayenne pepper
4 extra large egg whites

Preheat oven to 350°. Butter six, 3/4 cup soufflé dishes. Place 1 tablespoon Parmesan in each dish; rotate dishes to coat with cheese, leaving access in dishes. Place dishes on baking sheet. Whisk milk and yolks in bowl to blend. Melt butter in saucepan over medium-high heat. Add onion, thyme and rosemary; sauté 3 minutes. Add flour; whisk 1 minute. Whisk in milk mixture. Whisk soufflé base until thick and bubbling, about 2 minutes. Remove pan from heat. Add 1/2 cup goat cheese, salt, black pepper and cayenne pepper; whisk until cheese melts. Beat whites in bowl until stiff but not dry. Fold 1/4 of whites into base in pan. Sprinkle remaining 1/2 cup goat cheese and 1 tablespoon Parmesan over. Fold in remaining whites in two editions. Divide mixture among dishes. Bake soufflé is until puffed and beginning to brown on top, about 20 minutes. Serve immediately. Serves 6.

BRAISED LAMB SHANK WITH ROASTED PARMESAN FENNEL

4 Lamb shanks
3 tablespoons unsalted butter
2 tablespoons extra virgin olive oil
2 large red onions, coarsely chopped
2 large carrots, 2 peeled and coarsely chopped, 4 peeled and sliced into rounds
1 head of garlic, peeled, cut horizontally in half
8 large fresh thyme sprigs
1 1/2 pounds tomatoes, coarsely chopped
1 1/2 cups beef stock, or more
2 large fennel bulbs, quartered
1 bay leaf
1/4 cup Parmesan cheese

Preheat oven to 350°. Sprinkle lamb with salt and freshly ground black pepper. Melt 1 tablespoon butter with 1 tablespoon oil in large ovenproof pot over high heat. Working in batches, add lamb to pot and sauté until browned on all sides, about 8 minute per batch. Transfer lamb to bowl. Add onions, to chopped carrots, halved head of garlic and 6 thyme sprigs to pot and sauté until onions are brown, about 7 minutes. Add tomatoes and stir 2 minutes. Return lamb and any accumulated juices to pot. Stir in 1 1/2 cups stock. Sprinkle with salt and pepper. Bring mixture to simmer. Cover pot tightly; transfer to oven and bake until lamb is very tender, adding up to 3/4 cup more stock if juices evaporate, about 2 hours 15 minutes. Using tongs, transfer lamb to medium bowl. Pour vegetable mixture from pot into strainer set over large bowl. Press on solids to extract as much vegetable pulp and pan juice as possible. Return strained pulp and juice to pot. Spoon off fat from surface. Return lamb to pot; bring mixture to simmer. Season to taste with salt and pepper. Melt 2 tablespoons butter with 1 tablespoon oil in large nonstick skillet over medium-high heat. Add sliced carrots, to thyme sprigs, and bay leaf and sauté until vegetables begin to soften, about 5 minutes. Meanwhile, butter fennel, and roast until tender, about 40 minutes, sprinkle with parmesan cheese and bake until gold. Serve with vegetables. Serves 4.

ROASTED CHICKEN WITH TOMATOES AND RED PEPPER

plum tomatoes, about 4 cups, halved
¼ cup extra virgin olive oil
7 garlic cloves, pressed
1 ¼ teaspoons dried crushed red pepper
2 tablespoons chopped fresh marjoram
2 whole, small chickens, about 2 pounds each

Preheat oven to 450°. Toss tomatoes, olive oil, garlic, crushed red pepper, and 1 tablespoon marjoram in large bowl. Place chicken on rimmed baking sheet. Pour tomato mixture over chicken, arranging tomatoes in single layer on sheet around chicken. Sprinkle generously with salt and pepper. Roast until chicken is cooked through and tomatoes are blistered, about 35 minutes. Transfer chicken to plates. Spoon tomatoes and juice is over. Sprinkle with remaining 1 tablespoon marjoram. Serves 4.

SAVOY CABBAGE, ONION AND MUSHROOMS TURNOVERS

2 ounces dried porcini mushrooms, sliced
1 pound unsalted butter
1 ½ pounds onions, chopped
3 ½ pounds Savoy cabbage, cored and shredded
salt and a generous amount of fresh cracked black pepper
Philo leaves, defrosted according to package directions
¾ cup fresh breadcrumbs, toasted, or use Panko

Soak the porcini in warm water until softened, 10 to 15 minutes. Drain through a strainer lined with paper towels. Reserve soaking water. Melt 1stick butter in a very large, heavy, stockpot over medium-high heat. Add onions and sauté until wilted and golden, 8 to 10 minutes. Add cabbage, cover and cook over medium heat for 15 minutes until cabbage begins to soften. Uncover and continue cooking until light brown, 20 to 25 minutes, adding about 1/2 to 1 cup of the reserved mushroom soaking liquid to the pan, stir up any browned bits on the bottom to prevent burning. Stir in porcini, season generously season with salt and plenty of freshly ground black pepper. Preheat oven to 375°. Line a baking pan with parchment paper. Melt the remaining butter. Place 2 sheets of Philo with long side vertical on a workspace. Brush lightly with butter and sprinkle on 1 tablespoon of the bread crumbs, or panko. Cut in half lengthwise from top to bottom. Scoop out about 1/2 cup of cabbage mixture and place it on the lower left edge. Fold in a triangle shape, as if folding a flag. Place on the pan, brush with butter and continue in the same manner, until you have 24, 5 ounce turnovers. Bake until crisp and golden brown, 25 to 30 minutes. Strudels may be kept warm in a 250° oven for a least 1 hour or reheated. Serves 12.

PARISIAN WALNUT DIJON CHICKEN

6 boneless skinless chicken breasts
2 tablespoons unsalted butter, divided
1 clove garlic, minced
1/2 cup minced onion
2 ounces cream cheese
3/4 cup finely chopped walnuts
1/2 teaspoon salt
1/4 teaspoon fresh cracked black pepper
1/4 cup Dijon mustard, divided
1/2 cup half and half, or heavy cream, 40%
1/2 cup seeded, chopped tomatoes
2 tablespoons chopped fresh parsley
Sliced onions

Place chicken breasts between sheets of plastic wrap or waxed paper and flatten with a meat mallet until 1/4" thick. Melt 1 tablespoon butter in small sauté pan. Add garlic and minced onion; sauté until tender. Add cream cheese, walnuts, salt, and pepper. Sauté about 1 minute until blended. Divide mixture, reserving half for later use. Preheat broiler. Place about 1 tablespoon the walnut mixture on each breast; fold chicken over filling and place on baking pan. Reserve 1 tablespoon Dijon mustard. Brush remaining mustard on both sides of chicken. Broil 4 to 6 inches from heat source for 6 to 8 minutes per side or until done. Prepare sauce by combining remaining half of walnut mixture, reserved tablespoon of Dijon mustard, heavy cream, tomatoes, and parsley. Simmer on low heat until slightly thickened, about 2 to 3 minutes. Place chicken on platter; top with sauce and sautéed onions as garnish. Serves 6.

CRAB APPLE PICKLES WITH ROASTED VEAL LOIN

Crab apple pickles
1/4 cup plus 2 tablespoons extra virgin olive oil
juice of 2 limes
1 medium red onion, thinly sliced
3 tablespoons fresh thyme leaves
2- 1 3/4 pound of veal loin roasts, trimmed and tied at 2 inch intervals
freshly ground black pepper
salt

Pickels:
2 1/2 pounds crab apples with stem
6 cups white sugar
2 sticks cinnamon
1 1/2 tablespoon whole allspice
1 1/2 tablespoon whole cloves
3 cups each water & cider vinegar

Pierce apples. Ties spices in cheesecloth. Combine remaining ingredients and bowl in liquids for 5 minutes. Add apples and cook till tender.

In a large pot, combine the 1/4 cup of olive oil, and lime juice, onion and thyme. Season the veal with pepper, add it to the pot and seal. Turn to coat the veal with the marinade. Refrigerate for at least 8 hours. Bring to room temperature before roasting. Preheat the oven to 350°. Remove the veal from the marinade. Season with salt and pepper. Heat the remaining 2 tablespoons of olive oil into large skillet. Add the veal loins and cook over moderately high heat until browned all over about 5 minutes. Transfer the loins to a large roasting pan, leaving as much room between them as possible and roast for 1 hour, or until internal temperature at thickest part registers 140°. Transfer to a carving board and let rest for 10 minutes. Serve with crab apples and liquid. Serves 8.

HALIBUT WITH POTATOES AND OLIVES

1 ½ pounds a baking potatoes, peeled and sliced 1/8″ thick
¼ cup plus 1 tablespoon extra virgin olive oil
¼ cup coarsely chopped flat leaf parsley, plus 2 parsley sprigs
1 tablespoon finely chopped fresh rosemary
salt and freshly ground pepper
20 cherry or grape tomatoes, halved
1 cup Gaeta olives, 5 ounces
1 ½ pound halibut
2 thyme sprigs
1 cup dry white wine

Preheat the oven to 400°. In a large roasting pan, toss the potatoes with 2 tablespoons of the olive oil, the chopped parsley and the rosemary; season with salt and pepper. Spread the potatoes in an even layer. Scatter the tomatoes and olives over the potatoes and drizzle with 2 tablespoons of the olive oil. Season the fish with salt and pepper and stuff the parsley and thyme sprigs around it. Lay the fish on the potatoes and pour the wine over it. Rub the surface of the fish with remaining 1 tablespoon of olive oil and season with salt and pepper. Cover the roasting pan with foil and bake the fish for 15 minutes, or until almost cooked through. Discard the foil and baste the fish with the pan juices. Bake the fish for about 20 minutes longer, or until it is cooked through and the potatoes are tender. To serve, transfer the fish to a work surface. Transfer the potatoes, tomatoes and olives to a platter and set the fillets on top of the potatoes. Pour the pan juices over the fish and serve. Serves 6.

PORK LOIN WITH SAUSAGE GRAVY

3 tablespoons unsalted butter
3 tablespoons all-purpose flour
½ cup minced yellow bell pepper
¼ cup red onion, minced
1 ½ cups chicken stock
½ cup, 1/4″ cubes smoked sausage
¼ teaspoon cayenne pepper

2 tablespoons ground cumin
2 tablespoons ground coriander
1 teaspoon salt
½ teaspoon fresh ground black pepper
2 ½ pounds pork loin
3 tablespoons extra virgin olive oil
2 tablespoons minced fresh parsley

Preheat oven to 400°. Melt butter in heavy small saucepan over medium low heat. Add flour; cook until mixture is dark golden brown, stirring frequently, about 20 minutes. Add bell pepper and onion; sauté 3 minutes. Gradually whisk in stock. Add sausage and cayenne; increase heat and simmer 5 minutes, stirring often. Season with salt and pepper. Mix cumin, coriander, salt and pepper in medium bowl. Dredge pork in spices. Heat oil in heavy large ovenproof skillet over medium-high heat. Add pork and brown on all sides, about 8 minutes. Transfer skillet to oven; roast pork until thermometer registers 160°, about 10 minutes. Transfer to cutting board. Let stand five minutes. Slice pork 1/2” thick. Re- warm gravy. Mix in parsley. Pour gravy over pork and serve. Serves 6

PORTOBELLO SHORTRIBS AND ROASTED GARLIC MASHED POTATOES

4 portobello mushroom caps, marinated
 in olive oil and balsamic vinegar
1 ½ cups of boiling water
2 teaspoons chopped fresh thyme
1 teaspoon chopped fresh rosemary
1 teaspoon salt
1 teaspoon fresh ground black pepper
4 pounds meaty short ribs
2 tablespoons olive oil
1 large onion, chopped
1 medium carrot, peeled, chopped
3 large garlic cloves, minced
1 ½ ounces prosciutto, finely chopped
1 cup dry white wine
2 cups chicken stock
1 bay leaf
2 tablespoons, room temperature
2 cups breadcrumbs, or Panko
¼ cup stoneground mustard

Preheat oven to 350°. Mix 1 teaspoon thyme, rosemary, salt and pepper in small bowl. Rub mixture all over short ribs. Heat oil in heavy large ovenproof pot over medium-high heat. Working in batches, add ribs to pot and cook until brown on all sides, about 10 minutes per batch. Transfer ribs to bowl. Pour off all but two tablespoons fat from pot. Reduce heat to medium. Add onion, carrot, garlic and prosciutto, and marinated Portobello mushrooms to pot; sauté until vegetables begin to soften, about 5 minutes. Add wine and bring to boil, scraping up any browned bits from bottom of pot. Add broth, bay leaf and remaining 1 teaspoon thyme to pot. Return ribs to pot, meat side down; bring to boil. Cover pot tightly; transfer to oven and bake until ribs are very tender, about one hour 45 minutes. Remove from oven. Preheat oven to 450°F.

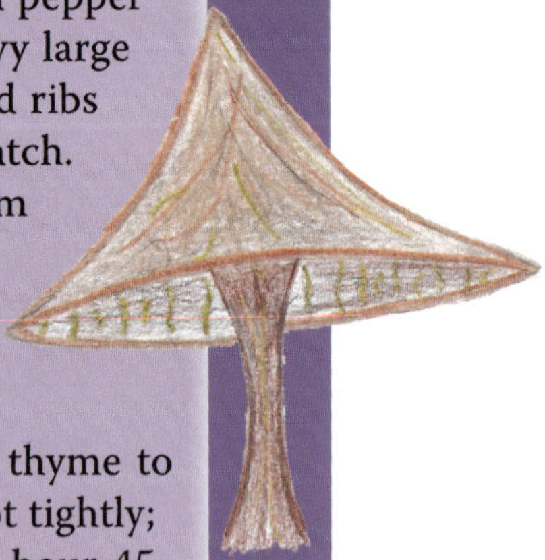

Transfer ribs two large roasting pan, boned side down. Remove 1 large mushroom cap from pot and finely chop. Place in medium bowl. Add butter and mix with fork to blend. Mix in bread crumbs or Panko. Season with salt and pepper. Spread 1 teaspoon mustard over top of each rib. Spread bread crumb mixture over top of each rib, pressing to adhere. Bake until topping is crisp and golden, about 10 minutes. Meanwhile, spoon off any fat from top of sauce in pot and discard. Boil sauce until slightly thickened, reduced to 2 cups. Slice remaining mushroom caps and place on top of ribs. Serve with roasted garlic mashed potatoes.

CREAMY MONKFISH AND MUSSELS STEW

1 stick, 4 ounces, unsalted butter
1 pound non-oily fish bones
4 shallots, thinly sliced
1 celery rib, chopped
1 carrot, coarsely chopped, plus 2 carrots, halved crosswise and cut into matchsticks
6 thyme sprigs
2 teaspoons coarse salt
1 teaspoon peppercorns
4 cups cold water
¾ cup dry white wine
¾ pound celery root, peeled and cut into matchsticks
2 leeks, white and tender green, cut into 1 1/2″ long matchsticks
salt and freshly ground pepper
1 cup heavy cream, 40%
2 tablespoons plus 2 teaspoons cornstarch dissolved in ¼ cup cold water
2 ½ pounds of monkfish fillet, cut into 1 1/2″ pieces
1 pound mussels, scrubbed and debearded

In a large saucepan, melt 4 tablespoons of the butter over moderate heat. Add the fish bones, shallots, celery, chopped carrot, thyme, salt and peppercorns and cook over low heat for 10 minutes. Add the water and wine and simmer for 30 minutes. Meanwhile, in a large skillet, melt the remaining 4 tablespoons of butter over moderate heat. Add the celery root, leeks and carrot matchsticks, cover and cook, stirring often, until softened, about 5 minutes. Season with salt and pepper and set aside. Strain the fish stock into a large saucepan. Whisk in the heavy cream and then dissolved cornstarch and bring to a simmer, whisking until thickened. Season with salt and pepper. Add the monkfish and the reserve vegetables and set the mussels on top. Cover and cook until the mussels open, 8 to 10 minutes. Serve in soup plates or bowls. Serves 4.

SOFT SHELL CRABS WITH WILTED ARUGULA

½ cup all-purpose flour
Salt and freshly ground black pepper
8 medium soft shell crabs, cleaned
2 tablespoons unsalted butter
¼ cup extra virgin olive oil
6 ounces baby are arugula, 8 loosely packed cups
2 ounces thinly sliced Sereno ham or prosciutto
lemon wedges, for serving

Season the flour with salt and pepper; dredge the crabs in the flour, tapping off any excess. In a large skillet, melt 1 tablespoon of the butter in 1 tablespoon of the oil. Add 4 of the crabs to the skillet and cook over moderately high heat until golden, about 3 minutes per side. Transfer the crabs to a low oven and keep warm. Repeat with another tablespoon each of the butter and oil in the remaining crabs. Wipe out the skillet. Add the remaining 2 tablespoons of oil and heat until shimmering. Add the arugula and season lightly with salt. Remove from the heat and toss quickly to barely wilt the arugula. Arrange the ham slices on plates and topped with the crabs. Mound the arugula along side and serve with lemon wedges. Serves 4.

SAUCES

"Every good cook should have a copper pot..."
- Martha Stewart

BERNAISE SAUCE

1 small shallot, minced
3 small fresh tarragon sprigs, leaves and minced and stems reserved
$\frac{1}{2}$ cup, 4 ounces, white wine vinegar
3 large egg yolks
$\frac{3}{4}$ cup, 6 ounces, unsalted butter, melted and kept warm
salt and freshly ground white pepper
1/8 teaspoon Worcestershire sauce
1 $\frac{1}{2}$ tablespoons fresh squeezed lemon juice

In a small, heavy saucepan, combine the shallot, tarragon stems, and vinegar. Bring to a simmer over medium low heat and cook until reduced to about 1 tablespoon, 4 to 5 minutes. Remove the mixture from the heat, let stand for 5 minutes, and then discard the tarragon stems. Whisk in the egg yolks, return the pan to low heat, and cook, whisking constantly until the mixture begins to thicken, 2 to 4 minutes. Remove from the heat and whisk in the butter 1 tablespoon at a time, whisking in a thoroughly before adding more. After the first few tablespoons of butter have been incorporated, return to the heat and add the rest more quickly. When all the butter has been added and the sauce is smooth and glossy, remove from the heat again and whisk in 1/4 teaspoon salt, 1/8 teaspoon white pepper, the Worcestershire sauce, the lemon juice, and the minced tarragon. Adjust the seasoning with salt and white pepper. Serve within 5 minutes, or cover and keep warm for up to 30 minutes in the top of a double boiler over hot, but not simmering, water.

HOLLANDAISE SAUCE

3 large egg yolks
salt and freshly ground white pepper
1 ice cube, if needed
½ cup, 4 ounces, unsalted butter, melted and kept warm
2 to 3 teaspoons fresh squeezed lemon juice, or to taste

In a small, heavy saucepan, combine 3 tablespoons water, the egg yolks, and 1/4 teaspoon salt. Cook over low heat, whisking constantly, until the mixture is foamy, 1 to 2 minutes. Continue whisking constantly until the mixture is pale yellow and begins to thicken, 1 to 2 minutes longer. Once it has thickened, do not heat it too quickly or it will curdle. If it appears granular, quickly remove it from the heat, drop in the ice cube, and whisk it in thoroughly. When the mixture is smooth with a glossy sheen, return the pan to the heat as soon as you begin to see the bottom of the pan as you whisk, remove from the heat. Whisk in the butter 1 tablespoon at a time, whisking in thoroughly before adding more. Whisk in 2 teaspoons lemon juice and taste. You should be able to taste the lemon, but the sauce should not be sour. Add more lemon juice, a drop or two at a time, if necessary. Season to taste with salt and white pepper. Serve within 5 minutes, or cover and keep warm for up to 30 minutes in the top of a double boiler over hot, but not simmering, water.

BORDELAISE SAUCE

1 ½ pound beef marrow bones, cut into 1 1/2 inch lengths by a butcher
2 teaspoons unsalted butter
1 large shallot, minced
1 ¼ cups, 10 ounces, dry red wine
1 fresh thyme sprig
1 bay leaf
½ cup, 4 ounces, veal demiglace
salt and freshly ground black pepper
1 tablespoon chilled unsalted butter, cut into 2 pieces

Put the marrow bones in a bowl filled with ice water and refrigerate for 20 minutes. Using your thumb, push the marrow out of the bones. If it won't move, immerse the bones in warm water for about 30 seconds and try again. Cut the marrow into 1 1/2 inch disks and cover with fresh ice water and refrigerate for 2 to 6 hours. In a saucepan over low heat, melt the butter. Add the shallots and cook until translucent, about 5 minutes. Add the wine, thyme, and bay leaf, raise the heat to medium, and let simmer briskly until reduced by about 3/4, 12 to 15 minutes. Remove and discard the herb's, and stir in the veal demiglace and 1/4 teaspoon each salt and pepper. Simmer, stirring occasionally, until slightly syrupy, 3 to 4 minutes. Turn off the heat, cover, and let stand. Drain the marrow discs and add them to the sauce. Warm the sauce and marrow over low heat, about 3minutes. Remove the pan from the heat and whisk in the chilled butter until it melts in the sauce thickens slightly.

BEURRE BLANC

2/3 cup, 5 ounces, dry white wine
2 tablespoons white wine vinegar or champagne vinegar
1 large shallot, minced
salt and freshly ground white pepper
1/3 cup unsalted butter, at room temperature, cut into 6 pieces
2 tablespoons finely chopped fresh chives

In a small saucepan over medium-high heat, combine the wine, vinegar, and shallot and bring to a boil. Reduce the heat to low and simmer gently until reduced to about one tablespoon, about 12 minutes. Watch carefully, so the liquid does not completely evaporate. Remove from the heat. Return the wine mixture to low heat. Add the 1/3 cup butter all at once and whisk constantly until the butter melts and is emulsified. Add 1/4 teaspoon each salt and white pepper, and the 2 tablespoons chives and whisk again.

CHOCOLATE BARBECUE SAUCE

½ up brewed strong coffee
½ cup ketchup
¼ cup apple cider vinegar
½ cup unsulphored molasses
2 large garlic cloves, minced
1 small red onion, minced
1 ounce, 1 square, unsweetened chocolate

Combine all ingredients except the chocolate in a small saucepan and bring to a boil over medium heat, stirring frequently. Reduce the heat and simmer gently for 30 minutes, until the sauce is reduced and thickened. Add chocolate and cook, stirring often, until the chocolate is melted, 2 to 3 minutes. Set aside until ready to serve.

BROWN BUTTER AND CAPER SAUCE

1/3 cup unsalted butter, at room temperature, plus2 tablespoons chilled unsalted butter cut into 4 pieces

¼ cup, 2 ounces, capers, preferably salt packed, rinsed

2 tablespoons good quality balsamic vinegar

2 tablespoons minced fresh flat leaf Italian parsley

1/4-1/2 teaspoon fresh squeezed lemon juice

Melt the 1/3 cup of butter in saucepan. As soon as it begins to turn dark brown, do not let it burn, remove the pan from the heat and carefully add the capers and vinegar, add the 2 tablespoons butter and parsley and swirl the pan just until the butter melts and the sauce is slightly thickened. Stir in 1/4 teaspoon lemon juice and taste for acidity; add the remaining juice, if desired.

SPICY LEMON AND PAPRIKA AIOLI

1 ½ cups good-quality mayonnaise
¼ cup fresh squeezed lemon juice
6 large garlic cloves, minced
1 ½ tablespoons tomato paste
1 ½ teaspoons hot smoked Spanish paprika
¼ teaspoon cayenne pepper

Combine all ingredients in small bowl; whisk to blend. Season aioli to taste with salt and pepper. Makes about 1 ¾ cups.

PORT AND DRIED CHERRY SAUCE

1 cup, Ruby port

2/3 cup dried cherries or cranberries, soaked in water for 20 minutes and drained

½ cup chicken stock

¼ teaspoon or red wine vinegar

1 teaspoon minced fresh rosemary

salt and freshly ground black pepper

2 tablespoons unsalted butter, cut into 4 pieces

Heat a pan to medium heat, and make the port and dried cherry sauce: carefully add the port and cherries to the pan. Bring to a simmer and deglaze the pan, scraping up bits from the bottom and sides, and cook until the liquid is reduced by half, about 2 minutes. Add the stock, vinegar, rosemary, 1/4 teaspoon salt, and a pinch of pepper and simmer until the sauce is slightly syrupy, about 2 minutes. Taste and adjust the seasoning. Remove the pan from the heat. Add the butter, and swirl the pan until the butter melts and the sauce is slightly thickened, about 30 seconds.

ESPRESSO BARBEQUE SAUCE

1 large onion, finely chopped
2 large garlic cloves, minced
¾ cup packed dark brown sugar
1 cup red wine vinegar
1 cup ketchup
1 cup brewed espresso
3 tablespoons molasses
2 tablespoons dry mustard mixed with one tablespoon water
½ cup ancho chili powder
2 tablespoons Worcestershire sauce
2 tablespoons ground cumin
1 teaspoon coarse salt
1 teaspoon freshly ground black pepper

Combine all ingredients and a medium saucepan and simmer over moderately low heat, stirring occasionally, until the sauce has reduced by about half, about 45 minutes. Let cool completely, strain, then purée in a food processor until smooth. Serve right away or cover and refrigerate until ready to use. This barbecue sauce may be refrigerated in a jar for up to 3 months. Makes about 2 cups.

MAYONNAISE

2 egg yolks
¾ teaspoon salt
½ teaspoon ground mustard
1/8 teaspoon white granulated sugar
Pinch cayenne pepper
4 -5 teaspoons fresh squeezed lemon juice
1 ½ cups extra virgin olive oil
4 teaspoons hot water

Place yolks, salt, mustard, sugar pepper and 3 teaspoons lemon juice in food processor. Process until blended. With motor running, slowly drizzle in ¼ cup olive oil. As mixture begins to thicken, continue adding oil in a fine steady stream, alternate with remaining lemon juice. Yields 1½ cups.

MAPLE-CHIPOTLE GLAZE

¾ cup pure maple syrup
¼ cup unsalted butter
4 garlic cloves, minced
6 teaspoons minced canned chipotle chilies
¼ teaspoon salt

Place all ingredients in saucepan and simmer over medium heat. Reduce hat to low and simmer until glaze is reduced to ¾ cup, stirring occasionally, about 10 minutes.

BLACK WALNUT AND FIG SPREAD

1 cup chopped stemmed dried Calimyrna figs
1/3 cup water
1/3 cup chopped pitted kalamata olives
2 tablespoons extra virgin olive oil
1 tablespoon drained capers, chopped
1½ teaspoons chopped fresh thyme
½ cup chopped black walnuts

Combine chopped figs and 1/3 cup water in heavy saucepan. Cook over medium heat until liquid evaporates and figs are soft, about 10 minutes. Transfer to medium bowl. Mix in the remaining ingredients, season to taste with salt and freshly ground pepper. Refrigerate and serve with goat cheese. 20 servings.

JAMS & JELLIES

HORSERADISH JELLY

3 ¼ cups white granulated sugar
½ cup prepared, not creamed horseradish
½ cup cider vinegar
½ cup liquid pectin

In a large pan heat and stir sugar, horseradish, and vinegar until sugar dissolves. Bring to boil, then stir in pectin all at once. Bring to full rolling boil while stirring, about 1 ½ minutes. Remove from heat and skim foam off top. Pour at once into hot sterilized jars and seal. Makes 6, 4 ounce jars.

ROASTED APPLE BUTTER

2 3/4 pounds McIntosh, or other tart apples, about 8, peeled, quartered and cored
2 cups cider

Preheat the oven to 450°. Arrange the apples and a large roasting pan. Pour the apple juice or the apples and bake for 30 minutes, or until tender and brown. Lower the oven to 350°. Using a fork or potato masher, thoroughly mash the apples in the roasting pan. Bake the apple purée, stirring occasionally, for 1 1/2 to 1 3/4 hours, or until very thick and deeply browned. Scrape into a bowl and let cool. Serve at room temperature or chilled. Makes about 3 cups.

GINGER RHUBARB JAM

4 cups diced fresh rhubarb
3 cups white granulated sugar
3 tablespoons chopped candied ginger
2 tablespoons fresh squeezed lemon juice

Place all ingredients in large sauce pan. Simmer until thick. Seal in jelly jars. Makes 6, 4 ounce jars.

PAPAYA JAM

3 pound firm-ripe papaya
3 cups white granulated sugar
½ cup fresh squeezed lemon juice or orange juice
Dash of salt

Wash papaya, cut in halves. Scoop out seeds and discard. Scoop flesh into bowl or pan and mash with a fork or potato masher. Measure out 3 cups. Place crushed pulp into a large pan. Add sugar and juice. Simmer together, sitting occasionally to keep mixture from scorching, until it passes the jam test. This will take about 1 hour. Ladle jam into hot containers and seal immediately. The jam will thicken slightly as it cools. Fills 36 ounces.

JENNIFERS JAMAICAN JAM

3 pounds ripe bananas

2 pound white granulated sugar

1¼ cups water

2 large lemons

1 large lime

½ teaspoon ground cinnamon

2/3 cup dark rum

Pinch cayenne pepper

Peel the bananas, cut into slices and place in pot. Add water and sugar and heat to dissolve sugar. Zest lemons and lime and add. Squeeze lemons and lime into mixture. Stir in cinnamon. Cook until thick, stirring frequently to prevent sticking and boiling over. Once thickened, take off heat and stir in rum. Process in jars and seal tightly. (slightly different quantities from each batch due to ripeness of bananas).

APRICOT ALMOND JAM

1 pound dried apricots

6 1/4 cups water

Juice of 2 lemons

Zest of 1 lemon

2 pound white granulated sugar

Handful of sliced almonds, toasted

Soak the apricots overnight in the water. Drain the fruit, reserving the liquid and puree in food processor. Put the apricots, soaking water, lemon juice and zest into a heavy pot and simmer for 20 minutes, stirring from time to time. Add the sugar and stir until dissolved. Then boil rapidly, stirring frequently to prevent the jam from sticking, until the sheeting stage is reached, about 10-15 minutes. Stir in almonds. Seal in sterilized jars.

JALAPENO PEPPER JELLY

4 large green bell pepper, seeded and chopped
4 jalapeno peppers, leave seeds in, chopped
1/3 cup water
5 pounds white granulated sugar
3 cups cider vinegar
3 packages (3 ounce), Certo
Green food coloring

Process peppers with water until smooth in food processor. In a very large saucepan, combine peppers, sugar and vinegar. Stir until dissolved. Boil for 4 minutes (watch close, this mixture boils over very fast). Remove from heat and stir in Certo and food coloring. Stir well until all is combined. Pour into hot sterilized jars. Seal and process in boiling water bath for 10 minutes. Yields 8, 8 ounce jars.

HONEY LEMON JELLY

6 large lemons
2 ½ cups clover honey or other "sweet fragrant" honey
3 ounce liquid pectin

Grate zest from lemons. Measure ¾ cup fresh squeezed lemon juice, discard seeds, keep pulp. Combine zest, juice and honey in saucepan, stirring well. Bring mixture to boil over medium heat, stirring constantly. Stir in pectin and return to a rolling boil, and boil for 1 minute. Remove from heat and pour jelly into sterilized jars. Process jars in boiling water bath for 5 minutes. Yields 4 half pints.

BASIL JELLY

1 quart water
2 cups firmly packed fresh basil leaves, finely chopped
1 package powdered fruit pectin
Green food coloring
5 cups sugar

In a large saucepan, bring water and basil to a boil. Remove from the heat; cover and let stand for 10 minutes. Strain and discard basil. Return 3 2/3 cups liquid to the pan. Stir in pectin and food coloring. Return to a rolling boil over high heat; skim off any foam. Pour hot liquid into hot jars, leaving ¼ inch space. Process for 15 minutes in water bath. Yields 6 half pints.

Basil aids in the healing of digestive disorders

CARAMELIZED ONION JAM

4 whole garlic bulbs

1 teaspoon extra virgin olive oil
5 cups chopped Vidalia onion
¼ cup unsalted butter, cold, cubed
¾ cup apple cider vinegar
1½ teaspoons ground mustard
1 teaspoon salt
¾ teaspoons freshly ground white pepper
½ teaspoon ground ginger
¼ teaspoon ground cloves
6 cups white granulated sugar
1 pouch (3 ounces) liquid fruit pectin

Remove outer (paper) from garlic. Do not separate cloves. Cut the tops off garlic bulbs; brush with oil. Wrap each bulb in aluminum foil. Bake in preheated 425F oven for 35 minutes or until roasted and softened. Cool for 15 minutes. In large skillet, sauté onion in butter for 30 – 40 minutes or until lightly browned. Squeeze roasted garlic into pan. Stir in cider vinegar, mustard, salt, pepper, ginger, and cloves. Bring to a rolling boil. Gradually add sugar, stirring constantly. Return to a boil for 3 minutes. Add pectin; bring to a full rolling boil. Boil for 1 minute, stirring constantly. Remove from heat, let stand 3 minutes, remove any foam that has formed. Pour into jars. And process in water bath for 10 minutes. Yields 3 ½ pints.

BREADS

CHIVE AND HONEY CORNBREAD

1 2/3 cups bread flour

1 1/3 cups stoneground white cornmeal

1 ½ tablespoons baking powder

1 teaspoon salt

2 extra large eggs

1 1/3 cups whole milk

½ cup corn oil

1/3 cup clover or lavender honey

½ cup finely snipped chives

Preheat the oven to 350°. Oil and 9 x 13 inch metal baking pan. In a bowl, sift the flour with the cornmeal, baking powder and salt. In a large bowl, whisk the eggs with the melt, corn oil and honey. Gently stir the dry ingredients and chives into the egg mixture until blended. Scrape the batter into prepared pan and bake for about 20 minutes or until the cornbread is golden and springs back when gently pressed. Let cool in the pan, and cut into squares and serve. Serves 8.

PANCETTA BISCUITS
WITH ROASTED APPLE BUTTER

12 slices pancetta, sliced thin
3 cups all-purpose flour
1 ½ teaspoons kosher salt
1 ½ teaspoons baking powder
¾ teaspoon baking soda
1 ½ cups heavy cream, 40%

In a large skillet, cook the pancetta over moderate heat until crisp, about 10 minutes. Drain on paper towels, crumble. Pour the bacon fat into a small bowl and let cool; refrigerate until solid. Preheat the oven to 400°. In a bowl, whisk the flower with salt, baking powder and baking soda. Add 5 tablespoons of the cold bacon fat. Use your fingers to gently blend it with flour until the mixture resembles coarse meal. Stir in the cream until a loose dough forms. Scrape onto a lightly floured surface and knead gently until smooth. Roll out the dough to a 10 x 12 inch rectangle about 1/2" thick. Cut into 2 1/4" squares and transfer to an ungreased baking sheet. Bake the biscuits for 25 minutes, or until golden, let cool slightly on a wire rack and serve with roasted apple butter. Makes about 20 biscuits.

SHREDDED WHEAT BREAD

2 cups boiling water
2 large shredded wheat biscuits, plain
1 teaspoon salt
1/3 cup granulated white sugar
1/3 cup unsulphored molasses
3 tablespoons shortening

2 packages yeast
5 cups white flour, plus more for kneading

In medium bowl, combine water, shredded wheat salt, sugar, molasses and shortening. Stir to mix well and let stand until just warm. Add yeast and mix, then add flour. Mix well. Turn out on floured board and knead 10 minutes, adding flour to keep from sticking. Place dough in greased bowl and let stand covered until double in size, about 2 hours. Punch down and divide into 2 balls. Knead for 5 minutes and place in prepared, greased loaf pans. Let rise covered until doubled, about 1 hour. Bake in preheated oven 375F for 35-40 minutes. Tapping on top should sound hollow. Turn out on rack to cool completely. Makes 2 loaves.

ANADAMA BREAD

1 ½cups water
1 teaspoon salt
1/3 cup yellow corn meal
1/3 cups unsulphored molasses
1 ½ tablespoon shortening
1 package yeast, dissolved in ¼ cup water
4 cups white flour, plus more for kneading

In a small sauce pan, bring to boil water and add salt. Reduce heat, at the simmering point, add corn meal, stir. Bring back to boil and add molasses, shortening. Take off heat and cool to lukewarm. When cool, add yeast mixture and stir. Add flour and combine, then turn out on floured board to knead 10 minutes. Turn into greased bowl and let rise double, about 1 hour. Punch down, turn out on lightly floured surface and knead 5 minutes. Separate into 2 balls, shape into loaves and turn into prepared greased loaf pans. Cover and let rise until double, about 1 hour. Bake in preheated 375F oven for 35 minutes, or until top sounds hollow when tapped. Turn out on rack to cool completely. Makes 2 loaves

BLACK WALNUT SCONES WITH FRESH CRANBERRY

1 1/3 cups cake flour

3 tablespoons white granulated sugar

2 teaspoons baking powder

pinch of salt

3 tablespoons cold unsalted butter, cut into small pieces

1 cup fresh cranberries

½ cup chopped black walnuts

1/3 cup buttermilk

½ teaspoon pure vanilla extract

Preheat the oven to 425° and line a baking sheet with parchment paper. In a medium bowl, mix the flour with the sugar, baking powder and salt. Using a pastry blender, cut in the butter until the mixture resembles a fine crumbs. Gently stir in the cranberries and walnuts. In a small bowl, mix the buttermilk with the vanilla. Add to the dry ingredients and stir with a fork until just the dough comes together. Turn the dough out onto a lightly floured surface. Pat the dough into a round and cut into 8 wedges. With lightly floured hands, pat the wedges into 1/2" thick rounds. Set the rounds on the prepared baking sheet and bake for 12 to 14 minutes, or until the scones are puffed and pale golden. Transfer to a rack and cool slightly before serving. Makes 8 scones.

PARMESAN DINNER ROLLS

Note: the unbaked roles need to be refrigerated overnight.

1½ cups milk
11 tablespoons unsalted butter
2 tablespoons white granulated sugar
1 envelope active dry yeast
4 cups all-purpose flour, plus more for dusting
1 ½ teaspoons salt
¾ cup packed freshly grated Parmesan cheese
2 tablespoons finely chopped fresh flat leaf parsley
1 tablespoon finely chopped fresh thyme
1 tablespoon finely chopped fresh rosemary

In a medium saucepan, heat the milk with 3 tablespoons of the butter and the sugar until just the butter melts. Transfer to a large bowl and let cool slightly. Stir in the yeast and let stand until dissolved, about 5 minutes. Add the 4 cups of flour and the salt and stir until a soft sticky dough forms. Turn the dough out onto a lightly floured surface and knead until silky, about 4 minutes. Transfer the dough to a lightly oiled bowl, cover with plastic wrap and let rise in a warm spot until doubled in bulk, about 1 hour. In a small shallow bowl, mix the cheese with the parsley, thyme and rosemary. Melt the remaining 8 tablespoons of butter in a small saucepan. Lightly butter 18 of the cups in 2 or more nonstick muffin pans. Punch down the dough and divide it into 3 equal pieces. Working with 1 piece of dough at a time keep the rest covered, roll the piece of dough into 1 inch thick rope. Then cut the rope into 18 equal pieces; roll each piece into a ball.

Dip half of each ball into the remaining butter, and then into the herb cheese mixture and arrange for 3 balls in each prepared muffin cup, coated sides touching in the center. Repeat with the remaining dough and topping. Brush the top of the rolls with remaining melted butter. Cover the muffin pans with plastic wrap and refrigerate overnight. Remove from refrigerator. Loosely drape the plastic wrap over the muffin tins. Let the rolls rise in a warm spot until they are about 1 inch above the rim of the cups, about t2 hours. Preheat the oven to 425°. Bake the rolls in the lower and middle thirds of the oven for about 15 minutes, or until golden and sizzling; shift to pans halfway through from top to bottom and back to front for even browning. Turn the rolls out onto a rack and let cool slightly before serving. Makes about 1½ dozen rolls.

ALMOND POPPYSEED BREAD

3 cups flour
2 1/4 cups white granulated sugar
1 1/2 teaspoons baking powder
1 1/2 teaspoon salt
3 large eggs
1 1/2 cups whole milk
1 1/8 cup vegetable oil
1 1/2 teaspoon vanilla extract
1 1/2 tablespoon poppy seeds
1 1/2 teaspoon almond extract
1 1/2 teaspoon butter flavored extract

In a large mixing bowl, combine flour, sugar, baking powder and salt. In a separate mixing bowl, whisk together eggs, milk, oil vanilla, poppyseed, almond and butter flavored extract. Combine wet ingredients with dry ingredients, stir well. Grease and flour for small loaf pans, 2 ½ x 6 x 2 ½ . Pour batter into prepared pans, bake in preheated 350° oven 55 minutes.

CRANBERRY ORANGE BREAD

2 cups flour
½ cup white granulated sugar
1 tablespoon baking powder
1/2 teaspoon salt
grated zest of 1 large orange
2/3 cup fresh squeezed orange juice
2 extra large eggs, lightly beaten
6 tablespoons butter, melted
1 ¼ cup fresh cranberries
½ cup walnuts, chopped coarse

Preheat the oven to 350°. Grease loaf pan well. Sift the flour, sugar, baking powder, and salt into a mixing bowl. Stir in the orange zest. Make a well in the center and add the orange juice, eggs, and melted butter. Stir from the center until the ingredients are blended; did not over mix; add the cranberries and walnuts and stir until blended. Transfer the batter to the prepared pan and bake until a cake tester inserted in the center comes out clean, 15 minutes. Let cool in the pan for 10 minutes before transferring to a rack to cool completely. Makes 1 loaf, or 2 small loaves.

WHOLE WHEAT BANANA NUT BREAD

½ (1 stick), butter at room temperature
½ cup white granulated sugar
2 extra large eggs, at room temperature
1 cup all-purpose flour
1 teaspoon baking soda
1 teaspoon ground cinnamon
Pinch of cayenne pepper
¼ teaspoons salt
½ cup whole wheat flour
3 large ripe bananas
1 teaspoon vanilla extract
½ cup pecans, chopped coarse

Preheat the oven to 350°. Grease the bottom and sides of a 9 x 5 inch loaf pan. With an electric mixer, cream the butter and sugar together until light and fluffy. Add the eggs, one at a time, beating well after each addition. Sift the all-purpose flour, baking soda, salt, cayenne and cinnamon over the butter mixture and stir to blend. Stir in the whole wheat flour. With a fork, mash the bananas to a purée, then stir into the batter. Stir in the vanilla and pecans. Pour the batter into the prepared pan. Bake until a cake tester inserted in the center comes out clean, 55 minutes. Let stand 10 minutes before transferring to a rack. Makes 1 loaf, or 2 small loaves.

IRISH SODA BREAD

4 cups flour

4 teaspoons baking powder

1 cup sugar

½ teaspoon caraway seeds

1 cup gold raisins

½ cup currants

2 eggs

½ cup cold butter

1 cup milk

Sift flour, baking powder, sugar and salt together. Sprinkle a little over the raisins and currants. Cut in the shortening with a pastry cutter or knife, then add eggs and milk. Turn onto floured surface and mold into round loaf, handle gently. Place in greased pan. I like to us my black cast iron frying pan, make sure it's well greased. Bake for 1 hour in 350F oven.

AVOCADO BREAD

2 cups white flour
½ teaspoon baking soda
¾ teaspoon baking powder
¼ teaspoon salt
¾ cup white granulated sugar
¾ cup chopped pecans
1 medium, ripe avocado
2 extra large eggs
½ cup buttermilk

In a large bowl, combine flour, baking soda, baking powder, salt, sugar and pecans. In separate bowl, mash avocado; add eggs and buttermilk and mix well. Add wet ingredients to dry ingredients and mix only until flour is moistened. Do not over mix. Pour batter into a greased 9 x 5 loaf pan, or 2 smaller pans and bake in preheated 350F oven for 50 minutes. Let cool in pan 5 minutes, then turn onto rack to cool completely.

CARROT NUT BREAD

2 cups grated carrots
3 cups white flour
1 teaspoon salt
1 teaspoon baking powder
¼ teaspoon baking soda
2 teaspoons cinnamon
3 extra large eggs
2 cups white granulated sugar
1 cup vegetable oil
1 teaspoon pure vanilla extract, or 1 whole vanilla bean stripped
½ cup whole milk
¾ cup chopped walnuts

Preheat the oven to 350F. Prepare two medium loaf pans by greasing and dusting with flour. Mix the flour, salt, baking powder, baking soda and cinnamon in a large bowl. White the eggs together in medium bowl. Stir in the sugar, then add the oil, vanilla and milk. Add wet ingredients to dry ingredients, along with carrots and nuts. Mix until just combined. Bake for 45 – 50 minutes. Transfer to racks to cool. Remove bread after 10 minutes.

HONEY CORN MUFFINS

¾ cup white flour
1 ¼ teaspoons baking powder
½ teaspoon salt
1/3 cup cornmeal
1 extra large egg, well beaten
1/3 cup whole milk
¼ cup chestnut honey
3 tablespoons, melted shortening
¼ cup peeled, diced tart apple

Sift flour with baking powder and salt. Stir in cornmeal. Combine egg, milk, honey and shortening. Stir in apple. Add all at once to dry mixture, stirring only until moistened. Fill greased muffin pans ¾ full. Bake at 400F for 20 minutes or until golden brown. Makes 8 muffins.

ENGLISH MUFFINS

1 cup whole milk
2 tablespoons white sugar
1 teaspoon salt
3 tablespoon unsalted butter, room temperature
1 cup hot water
1 package dry yeast
5 1/2 cups white flour
Corn meal
Oil for frying

Scald the milk; stir in sugar, salt and butter. Cool. Dissolve yeast in cup of hot water. Mix milk and water together. Add 3 cups flour and mix until smooth. Add 2 cups flour until dough forms a ball. Turn out on floured board and knead until smooth and elastic, about 10 minutes. Cover in a greased bowl and let rise double. About 1 hour. Punch down, return to lightly floured board and flatten out to ½ inch thick. Cut 3" rounds and place on cookies sheet sprinkled with cornmeal. Let rise double, about 2 hours. Fry in a minimum of oil in frying pan on medium heat, until golden. Cool on wire racks. Makes about 2 dozen.

PITA BREAD

1 package dry yeast
1 1/3 cup warm water
2 cups white flour
1 tablespoon vegetable oil
1 teaspoon white sugar
1 teaspoon salt
1-1½ cups whole wheat flour

Dissolve yeast in warm water and let stand 20 minutes. Combine all ingredients in large bowl and stir until moist. Turn out on floured surface and knead until smooth and elastic. Turn into greased bowl and cover in warm place and let rise until double, about 2 hours. Punch down and divide into 6 balls. Knead each ball another 10 minutes and place them on a lightly floured surface to rise double, about 1 hour. Punch down and roll out in 7" circles. Place on lightly greased cookie sheet to rise for 30 minutes, not double. Bake at 450F for 10 minutes and cool completely on rack. Makes 6 pitas.

ONION BREAD

1 package dry yeast
¼ cup warm water
1 package dry onion soup mix
1 cup water
2 tablespoons white sugar
1 cup small curd cottage cheese
1 teaspoon salt
¼ teaspoon baking soda
2 tablespoons shortening
4-5 cups white flour
1/3 cup toasted wheat germ
Corn meal

Dissolve yeast in ¼ cup warm water. Combine soup mix with 1 cup water and simmer 10 minutes. Add sugar, cottage cheese, salt, baking soda and shortening. Stir and cool until lukewarm. Stir in 2 cups flour, beat well. Stir in yeast mixture. Add wheat germ and enough flour to make a stiff dough. Cover and let rise 1 ½ hours. Punch down and return to lightly floured surface, divide into 2 loaves. Knead another 10 minutes and place in greased loaf pans dusted with corn meal. Cut diagonal slits in top and let rise 1 hour more. Bake in 375F oven for 20 minutes. Brush with egg white and 1 tablespoon water for 10 minutes longer. Remove from pan and cool completely. Makes excellent dinner rolls. Yields 2 loaves.

VEGETABLES & SIDES

SWEET CORN AND RADISH RELISH

6 cups fresh corn kernels
3/4 cup thinly sliced radishes
6 tablespoons chopped fresh cilantro
3 1/2 tablespoons fresh squeezed lime juice
2 tablespoon white sugar
3 tablespoons extra virgin olive oil
2 green onions, chopped
2 tablespoons minced, seeded, jalapeno chilies

Combine all ingredients in a large bowl. Season with salt and freshly ground black pepper to taste. Serves 8.

JASMINE RICE
WITH EDAMAME AND TOMATO

2 cups water
1 ½ cups jasmine rice
1 cup chopped roma tomatos
1 pound boiled soybeans, edamame, shelled
1 tablespoon peanut oil
¾ teaspoons salt
1 ½ tablespoons sesame seeds, toasted

Combine 2 cups water, rice, soybeans, oil and salt in large saucepan. Bring to boil over high heat, stirring occasionally. Reduce heat to medium, cover and simmer until rice is tender, about 15 minutes. Remove from heat. Let stand, covered, 5 minutes. Fluff rice with fork. Stir in tomato and sesame seeds; season with salt and freshly ground black pepper. Serves 6.

TURNIP AND CARROT MASH WITH HONEY LEMON JELLY

1 1/4 pounds rutabagas, peeled, cut into strips
1 pound carrots, peeled, cut into strips
1/4 cup unsalted butter
1/4 cup fresh squeezed lemon juice
3 tablespoons clover honey
1 teaspoon grated a lemon zest
1/2 cup chopped fresh chives

Cook rutabagas in a large pot of boiling salted water 2 minutes. Add carrots and cook until vegetables are tender, about 6 minutes. Drain. Melt butter in large pot over medium-high heat. Add lemon juice, honey and zest. Bring to boil. Add vegetables; cook until glazed, stirring occasionally, about 6 minutes. Season to taste with salt and freshly ground black pepper. Remove from heat. Mix in fresh chives. Serves 8.

SUGAR SNAP PEAS AND GREEN BEANS

¼ cup extra virgin olive oil
2 tablespoons red wine vinegar
½ teaspoon salt
1 pound slender green beans, trimmed, cut in half on diagonal
1 pound white turnips,2-2 ½ inches, each cut into 16 wedges
1 cup fresh peas
2 tablespoons chopped fresh dill
2 tablespoons chopped fresh Italian parsley
2 tablespoons chopped fresh mint

Whisk oil, vinegar, and salt in medium bowl to blend. Cook green beans and turnips in a large pot of boiling salted water, or steam, until crisp tender, about 5 minutes. Drain. Transfer vegetables to bowl of ice water. Drain well. Heat vinaigrette in heavy large skillet over medium heat until warm. Add beans, turnips, and peas; toss until heated through and coated with the vinaigrette, about 5 minutes. Add all herbs and toss to coat. Season to taste with additional salt and freshly ground black pepper. Serves 8.

HONEY HORSERADISH CARROTS

5 pound carrots, cleaned, sliced on diagonal
2 teaspoons salt
1 stick unsalted butter
8 ounces prepared horseradish
½ cup honey
1 cup freshly chopped parsley
Salt and fresh ground black pepper

In a large pot, bring water to boil with salt. Add carrots and cook for 10 minutes, drain and plunge in ice bath to assure color and flavor. In a large skillet, melt butter oven medium high heat. Add carrots and horseradish. Cook until carrots are tender, but not over done, about 15 minutes. Add honey and stir to combine. Add parsley and season with salt and pepper to taste. Serves 8.

GREEN BEANS WITH GORGONZOLA

1 pound fresh green beans, washed and snipped
½ pound applewood smoked bacon
8 ounces gorgonzola cheese, crumbled
2 cups coarsely chopped walnuts
Freshly ground black pepper

Prepare beans and steam until just tender, but still snap, about 7 minutes. Meantime, cook bacon in a large skillet, cooking crisp. Remove bacon and chop coarse, reserve bacon fat. Return beans and bacon to skillet and toss with bacon fat. Add crumbled cheese and walnuts. Garnish with a generous amount of freshly ground black pepper. Serve when the cheese is softened. Serves 4.

ROOT VEGETABLE PANCAKES

2 pounds parsnips, peeled
1 pound carrots, peeled
1 teaspoon salt
½ cup chopped onion
¼ cup white flour
1 extra large egg, lightly beaten
1 tablespoon minced chives
Oil for frying

Place parsnips and carrots in a large saucepan and cover with water; add salt. Bring to a boil over medium high heat. Reduce heat; cover and cook for 15 – 20 minutes or until tender. Drain and place vegetables in a large bowl; mash. Stir in the onion, flour egg and chives. Drop batter by ¼ cupfuls onto a well greased hot griddle. Flatten with a spatula. Fry until golden brown; turn and cook until second side is lightly browned. Drain on paper towels. Seves 6.

ROASTED YAMS
WITH SWEET CURRY

2- 8 ounce red skinned sweet potatoes (yams), halved lengthwise

1 teaspoon extra virgin olive oil

1 teaspoon curry powder

1 cup plain yogurt

1 plum tomato, chopped

2 tablespoons chopped fresh cilantro

2 green onions

Preheat oven to 400F. Spray small baking sheet with nonstick spray. Drizzle cut sides of sweet potatoes with 1 teaspoon olive oil. Place potatoes, cut side down, on prepared sheet. Roasted until tender and brown about 30 minutes. Cool to room temperature. Stir curry powder in small skillet over medium low heat until fragrant, about 30 seconds. Remove from heat. Mix yogurt, tomato, fresh cilantro and curry powder in small bowl. Season to taste with sat and freshly ground black pepper. Serve sweet potatoes cold at room temperature topped with chilled yogurt topping and chopped green onions. Serves 4.

BELGIAN BISTRO FRIES WITH GARLIC

4 medium russet potatoes, cut into thick wedges
Oil for frying, twice
1/4 cups chopped fresh parsley
4 garlic cloves, minced
Coarse salt

Turn on fryers and preheat to 425F. Cut potatoes in 1/3 inch wedges. Pat potato strip dry with paper towels. Fry until potatoes are light golden brown. Remove from oil, let cool. Re-fry when cool to a deep gold brown. Transfer potatoes to bowl and toss with parsley, garlic and coarse salt.

LENTILS A DIFFERENT WAY

3 tablespoons extra virgin olive oil
1 cup finely chopped red onion
2/3 cup finely chopped carrot
½ cup finely chopped fennel
1 ¼ cups dried green lentils
4 cups chicken stock

Heat oil in heavy medium saucepan over medium high heat. Add onion, carrot and fennel and sauté until slightly softened, about 7 minutes. Add lentils and stir 1 minute. Add stock and bring to boil. Reduce heat to medium low; cover and simmer until lentils are just tender, stirring occasionally, about 35 minutes. Season with salt and freshly ground black pepper to taste. Serves 4.

ROASTED AUBERGINE WITH TOMATOES AND CILANTRO

2 medium eggplants, halved lengthwise
1/3 cup vegetable oil
2 large white onions
3 tablespoons finely chopped peeled ginger
1 pound tomatoes, coarsely chopped
2 teaspoons ground cumin
1 ½ teaspoons sweet paprika
1 teaspoon ground coriander
½ teaspoon cayenne pepper
1/3 cup chopped fresh cilantro

Preheat oven to 350F. Oil baking sheetpan; place eggplant halves, cut side down on sheet. Roast eggplant until flesh is soft, about 1 hour. Cool slightly. Using a spoon, scoop pulp from eggplant halves into medium bowl; mash. Discard skins. Heat oil in heavy large skillet over high heat. Add onion and sauté until brown and translucent, releasing their natural sugars, about 10 minutes. Add ginger and stir 2 minutes. Add tomatoes and next 4 ingredients; sauté 6 minutes to blend flavors. Add eggplant and stir until slight thickened, about 5 minutes. Remove from heat. Stir in cilantro. Season to taste with salt and freshly ground black pepper. Serve over rice. Serves 6.

Cilantro is an anti-inflammatory, and may relieve symptoms of arthritis…

TOMATO SLAW
WITH SHERRY VINIAGRETTE

1/3 cup sherry
5 tablespoons clover honey
2 tablespoons mustard seeds
2 tablespoons stoneground mustard
2/3 cup extra virgin olive oil
3 pounds thinly sliced red cabbage
10 green onions, sliced
2 pounds sliced plum tomatoes

Whisk first 4 ingredients in large bowl to blend. Gradually whisk in oil. Add cabbage, green onion, and tomatoes; toss to coat with vinaigrette. Season to taste with salt and freshly ground black pepper. Cover and refrigerate at least 2 hours. Makes 8 servings.

ROASTED SUCCOTASH WITH HERBS

3 tablespoons unsalted butter
3 tablespoons extra virgin olive oil
1 large red onion, chopped
1 red bell pepper, cut into ½ inch pieces
1 green bell pepper, cut into ½ inch pieces
1 garlic clove, minced
2 cups fresh corn kernels, from about 4 ears, roasted until charred
2 medium zucchini, trimmed, cut into ¾ inch pieces
2 medium sized yellow squash, cut into ¾ inch pieces
1 package lima beans
4 tablespoons chopped fresh Italian parsley
1 tablespoon chopped fresh marjoram

Melt butter with oil in heavy large deep skillet over medium heat. Add onion, both peppers and garlic; sauté until pepper are crisp tender. Add corn(to roast corn, soak in husks for 1 hour in water. Preheat grill on high. Lay corn on direct heat and turn frequently to avoid burning, roast until husk is charred evenly. Remove from heat, husk and slice kernels from cob into bowl), zucchini, yellow squash and lima beans, saute until vegetable are just tender, about 7 minutes. Stir in 3 tablespoons parsley and marjoram. Season to taste with salt and freshly ground black pepper. Makes 8 servings.

Marjoram aids in the relaxing of muscles…

HAPPY ENDINGS

AARON'S BAKLAWA

2 1/2 cups plus 1/3 cup white granulated sugar

1 1/2 cups water

1 tablespoon fresh squeezed lemon juice, without seeds or pulp

1 1/2 cups (3 sticks) unsalted butter, melted

1 pound shelled pecans, coarsely chopped

18 phyllo pastry sheets, about 1 pound

Stir 2 ½ cups sugar, 1 ½ cups water, and fresh squeezed lemon juice in medium saucepan over medium heat until sugar dissolves. Increase the heat and boil 5 minutes. Remove syrup from heat. Refrigerate until syrup is cold. Preheat oven to 325F. Brush 13x9x2 metal baking pan with some of the melted butter. Mix pecans and remaining 1/3 cup sugar in large bowl. Fold 1 sheet of phyllo in half to form 12 x 9 inch rectangle. Place folded sheet in prepared pan. Brush generously with melted butter. Repeat with 5 more sheets, brushing each generously with butter. Sprinkle half of the nut mixture over. Top with 6 more folded sheets, brushing with butter. Sprinkle remaining nut mixture over. Using sharp knife, make 5 diagonal cuts across phyllo, cutting through top layers only and spacing cuts evenly. Repeat in opposite direction to form diamond pattern. Bake baklawa until deep golden brown, about 1 hour. Slowly spoon 1½ cups cold syrup over hot baklawa; cover and chill remaining syrup. Recut baklawa along lines all the way through layers. Let stand 4 hours. Makes about 18 pieces.

SPICE POUNDCAKE

3 cups sifted all purpose flour
½ teaspoon baking powder
½ teaspoon baking soda
¼ teaspoon salt
2 teaspoon cinnamon
1 teaspoon cloves
1 cup soft, unsalted butter
2 cups white granulated sugar
4 extra large eggs
1 teaspoon pure vanilla extract
1 cup buttermilk

Preheat oven to 350F. Grease well and flour a bundt cake pan. Sift flour with baking powder, baking soda, salt, cinnamon, and cloves; set aside. In large bowl, with electric mixture at medium, beat butter with sugar until light. Add eggs and vanilla, beat until very light and fluffy. At low speed, beat in flour mixture, alternately with buttermilk. Beat only until combined. Turn into prepared pan. Bake 60-65 minutes, or until cake tester inserted in center comes out clean. Cool in pan, on wire rack, 15 minutes. Then turn out on rack; cool completely. Serves 18.

Vanilla is purported by ancient peoples that it could act like an aphrodisiac…

FLAN, TART AND TANGY

4 large white grapefruit
2 cups white granulated sugar
1 cup, packed, fresh mint leaves
3/4 cup whole milk
3/4 cup heavy cream, 40%
4 extra large eggs
1 teaspoon pure vanilla extract, or 1 whole vanilla bean scraped
salt

Cut peal and white pith from grapefruit. Working over bowl to catch juices, cut between membranes to release segments. Squeeze membranes to extract juice. Place segments in medium bowl. Transfer ½ cup grapefruit juice to heavy small saucepan. Reserve remaining juice. Add 1 cup sugar to juice in saucepan. Gently simmer until syrup thickens, stirring until sugar dissolves, about 5 minutes. Remove from heat. Stir in mint leaves. Cover and let steep 10 minutes. Strain syrup into bowl. Preheat oven to 325F. Combine ½ cup sugar and 2 tablespoons water in heavy small saucepan. Stir over medium heat until sugar dissolves. Increase heat and boil without stirring until deep amber, occasionally brushing down sides of pan with wet brush and swirling pan, about 8 minutes. Immediately divide caramel between six ¾ cup flan cups. Transfer cups to larger baking pan with water half way up sides of cups. Whisk ½ cup grapefruit juice, ½ cup sugar, milk, cream, eggs, vanilla and salt in large bowl until sugar dissolves. Divide mixture among prepared cups. Bake flans until just set, about 45 minutes. Cool flans in pan 1 hour. Remove from water, cover and chill at least 4 hours. Pour mint syrup over grapefruit segments. Using small sharp knife, cut around flans to loosen. Invert 1 flan onto each of 6 plates. Spoon grapefruit segments and syrup over flans. Serves 6.

SPICY CHOCOLATE WAFFLES

¾ cup sugar
½ cup vegetable oil
2 extra large eggs
1 teaspoon pure vanilla extract
1¼ cups white flour
6 tablespoons baking cocoa
1 teaspoon baking powder
½ teaspoon salt
½ teaspoon ground cinnamon
¼ teaspoon ground cayenne pepper

In a bowl, combine sugar, oil, eggs, and vanilla. Combine dry ingredients. Add to sugar mixture; mix well. Bake in preheated waffle iron according to manufacturers directions; remove carefully. Do not over bake. Serve warm with all your favorite sundae toppings. Serves 4.

PURELY DECADENT BROWNIES

1 cup, unsalted butter
1 1/4 cup semisweet chocolate chips
3 ounces unsweetened chocolate, chopped
1 cup plus 2 tablespoons white granulated sugar
3 extra large eggs
2 tablespoons espresso coffee granule
1 tablespoon pure vanilla extract
2/3 cup white flour
1 1/2 teaspoons baking powder
1/2 teaspoon salt
10 ounce package peanut butter chips
chopped salted peanuts

Preheat oven to 350F. Butter and flour 9 inch square metal baking pan. Combine butter, semisweet chocolate ships and unsweetened chocolate in heavy medium saucepan. Stir over low heat until chocolate mixture is melted and smooth. Remove from heat. Whisk 1 cup plus 2 tablespoons sugar, 3 eggs, espresso coffee and vanilla in large bowl until just combined. Add warm chocolate mixture: whisk to combine. Cool just to room temperature. Whisk 2/3 cup flour, baking powder and salt in medium bowl. Whisk into chocolate mixture. Mix in peanut butter chips and peanuts. Pour batter into prepared pan. Bake 35 minutes. Cool completely before cutting. Makes 9 large brownies.

BIKER'S SPORTS BAR

3 cups puffed cereal, Kashi
½ cup walnuts
¼ cup chopped pitted dates
¼ cup chopped dried cherries
¼ cup dark raisins
1/3 cup creamy peanut butter
¼ cup clover honey
¼ cup light corn syrup

Preheat oven to 350F. Spray 9 inch square metal baking pan with nonstick spray. Mix cereal, walnuts, dates, cherries and raisins, in medium bowl. Combine peanut butter, honey and corn syrup in heave small saucepan. Bring to boil, whisking constantly until mixture bubble vigorously and thicken slightly, about 1 minute. Pour peanut butter mixture over cereal mixture in bowl; stir to blend. Transfer mixture to prepared pan; press to compact. Bake until just golden around edges, about 10 minutes. Cool completely. Cut into 1 x 2 inch bars. Makes abut 18 bars.

SWEET RAVIOLI

4 cups coarsely grated whole milk mozzarella cheese
15 ounces whole milk or ricotta cheese
1 cup grated Pecorino Romano cheese
2 teaspoons grated lemon zest
2 teaspoons grated lime zest
4 cups white flour
1/2 teaspoon salt
4 extra large eggs, beaten
1/4 cup unsalted butter, cut into 1/2" pieces, room temperature
1/2 cup plus 2 tablespoons room temperature water
oil for frying
chestnut honey

Mix all cheeses and lemon/lime zest in large bowl; set cheese mixture aside. Lightly flour two baking sheets. Mix flour and salt in another large bowl; mix in beaten eggs. Using fingertips, rub in butter a few pieces at a time until well blended. Add one half cup water; stir to blend, adding more water by tablespoonfuls if dough is dry. Knead in a bowl until dough comes together. Turn dough out onto floured surface; knead until smooth and elastic, about 10 minutes. Divide dough into 4 pieces. Roll out one piece on lightly floured surface to 1/8" thickness. Using 3 1/2" diameter biscuit cutter cut out rounds. Repeat with remaining dough pieces. Transfer half of dough rounds to prepared baking sheets. Place 2 tablespoons cheese mixture in the center of each dough round on baking sheets. Brush edges of dough rounds lightly with water. Cover with remaining dough rounds, pressing firmly on edges to seal. Prepare oven to 300°F. Pour enough oil into heavy large pot to reach a depth of 2 inches. Heat oil to 350°. Add 3 to 4 ravioli at a time to hot oil in pot and fry until golden, turning once, about 4 minutes. Transfer to paper towels to drain. Place ravioli on baking sheets and keep warm in oven while frying remaining ravioli. Place ravioli on platter. Drizzle with honey and serve hot. Makes about 24.

RUSTIC CHERRY TART

Crust

2 cups all- white flour

½ cup white granulated sugar

1 teaspoon salt

1 cup chilled unsalted butter, cut into 1/2″ pieces

1 extra large egg

Filling

1 cup cherry preserves

½ cup chopped dried sweet cherries, about 2 ½ ounces

½ teaspoon grated lemon zest

¼ teaspoon pure almond extract

¼ cup unsalted natural pistachios, chopped

Glaze

1 extra large egg

2 tablespoons whole melt

2 tablespoons white granulated sugar

For crust:

Combine flour, sugar and salt in processor; blend 5 seconds. Add butter and cut in, using pulsing turns, until mixture resembles fine meal. Add egg and process just until moist clumps form. Gather dough into balls; divide in half. Flatten each half into disk. Wrap in plastic and chill until firm enough to roll, about 1 hour.

For filling:

Position rack and bottom third of oven and preheat to 325°. Mix preserves, chopped cherries, zest and almond extract in medium bowl. Roll out one dough disk on lightly floured surface to eat 11 inch round. Transfer round to 9 inch diameter tart pan with removable bottom press dough gently into pan; trim overhang, even with top of pan sides. Spread filling in crust; sprinkle with pistachios. Roll out second dough disk on lightly floured surface to 11 inch round; cut into 3/4" wide strips. Arrange several strips, spaced 3/4" apart over filling. Top with more strips at slight angle, forming lattice. Press strip ends to edge of pan and, trim overhang. For glaze; beat egg and whole milk in small bowl to blend. Brush some of glaze over lattice; sprinkle with 2 tablespoons sugar. Bake tart until crust is golden brown and cherry filling is bubbling thickly, about 1 hour. Cool tart completely in pan on rack. Serves 8.

APPLE GRANITA WITH GINGER WHIPPED CREAM

6 cups apple cider
2/3 cup packed dark brown sugar
20 whole allspice
12 whole cloves
½ teaspoon ground cayenne pepper

Combine all ingredients in saucepan over medium heat until sugar dissolves. Remove from heat, cover and let steep 1 hour. Strain mixture into a metal baking pan. Freeze until edges begin to set, about 1 hour. Whisk; freeze again until mixture is slushy, about 1 hour. Whisk again to blend, well. Freeze without stirring until granita is frozen solid, at least 3 hours, or overnight. Using fork, scrape granita until entire mixture is a mass of crystals. Cover and freeze until ready to serve. Top with Ginger whipped cream.

GINGERED WHIPPED CREAM

½ cup chilled whipping cream
1 tablespoon packed dark brown sugar
2 tablespoons minced crystallized ginger
3 tablespoons finely minced, or shredded fresh ginger

Beat cream and sugar in medium bowl until peaks form. Fold in gingers. Cover and chill up to 4 hours. Makes about 1 cup.

ALMOND CHERRY-PEACH COMPOTE

1 cup sliced, toasted almonds

1 pound tart cherries, pitted

1 pound ripe peaches, pitted and peeled

1½ cup water

½ cup packed, golden brown sugar

Place all ingredients in heavy saucepan and bring to boil. Boil until fruit is broken down and mixture is thick. Cover and chill overnight. Serve cold or at room temperature.

GARY'S CHEESE CAKE

Crust:

1¼ cups sifted white flour

8 tablespoons unsalted butter, cold

1/3 dark brown sugar, packed

¼ teaspoon baking soda

Mix together and cut butter in to resemble coarse crumbs.
Press firmly into 9 inch spring form pan.

Filling:

24 ounces cream cheese

1 ½ cups white granulated sugar

4 extra large eggs

½ teaspoon pure vanilla extract or beans from 2 large vanilla pods

Blend cream cheese and sugar until fluffy. Add eggs, one at a time until smooth. Then add vanilla. Blend this together and pour on top of crust. Bake at 350F for 60 minutes or lightly brown on top. Cool completely on rack. Serves 12.

PEANUT BUTTER BARS

1 cup shortening
1 cup white granulated sugar
1 cup brown sugar packed
2 extra-large eggs
2/3 cup peanut butter, creamy
¼ teaspoon salt
¼ teaspoon baking soda
1 teaspoon vanilla, or one large vanilla bean stripped
2 cups white flour
2 cups oatmeal
1 large bag chocolate chips

Cream together shortening, sugar, and brown sugar. Blend in eggs, peanut butter, salt, baking soda, vanilla. Add flour and oatmeal. Press into the bottom of a 9 x 13 inch pan evenly, bake 18 minutes at 350°. When removing from oven, let cool 5 minutes, then spread entire bag of chocolate chips on top until melted. Cool completely. Makes 24 bars.

GINGER GINGERBREAD

Cake:

1¼ cups all-purpose flour

2 teaspoons ground ginger

1 teaspoon ground cinnamon

1 teaspoon baking soda

¼ teaspoon ground cloves

¼ teaspoon salt

¼ cup finely chopped crystallized ginger

½ cup vegetable oil

½ cup unsulphured molasses

½ cup, packed, dark brown sugar

1 extra large egg

1 ½ teaspoons grated lemon zest

½ cup boiling water

Preheat oven to 350°. Butter and flour 8 inch square metal baking pan. Whisk first six ingredients in medium bowl to blend well; whisk in crystallized ginger. Whisk oil, molasses and brown sugar in large bowl to blend; whisk in egg and lemon zest. Gradually whisk in dry ingredients, then boiling water. Transfer batter to prepared pan. Bake cake until tester inserted into center comes out clean, about 30 minutes. Serve with mascarpone cream. Serves 9.

MASCARPONE CREAM

8 ounces mascarpone cheese
3 tablespoons chestnut honey
2 tablespoon fresh squeezed lemon juice

Whisk cheese, honey and lemon juice in small bowl to blend. Cover; chill until ready to serve.

FRITTERS WITH HONEY

½ cup vanilla soy milk
1 teaspoon dry yeast
2 extra large egg yolks
2 tablespoons extra virgin olive oil
2 tablespoons white granulated sugar
2 tablespoons and dark rum
1 teaspoon salt
2 ½ cups white flour
oil for frying
½ cup lavender honey

Heat vanilla flavored soy milk in small saucepan over low heat until warmed to 110°. Pour soy milk into large bowl. Sprinkle dry yeast over; let stand until yeast dissolves, about 10 minutes. Mix in egg yolks, olive oil, sugar, dark rum and salt. Gradually mix in all-purpose flour by one half cupfuls. Knead dough in bowl until smooth, about 3 minutes. Cover bowl; let dough rest 30 minutes. Using floured hands, shape dough into 1 inch diameter balls. Add enough oil to heavy large deep saucepan to reach depth of 3 inches. Heat oil to 350°. Working in batches, fry 6 fritters at a time until golden brown, turning often, about 3 minutes. Using a slotted spoon, transfer to several layers of paper towels to drain. Place warm fritters and large bowl. Pour honey over. Stir to coat evenly. Makes about 30.

PUMPKIN PIE BRULEE

Piecrust dough:
1¼ cups all-purpose flour
¼ teaspoon salt
5 tablespoons chilled unsalted butter, cut into 1/2″ pieces
1 tablespoon white vinegar
¼ cup vegetable shortening
1 - 2 tablespoons ice water

Whisk flour and salt in medium bowl to blend. Add butter and shortening. Rub with fingertips until very course meal forms. Sprinkle with 1 tablespoons water and vinegar. Toss until moist clumps form, sprinkling with more water by teaspoonfuls if mixture is dry. Put dough into ball; flatten. Wrap and chill, at least 1 hour.

Brulee:
15 ounces pure pumpkin
¾ cup plus 4 tablespoons white granulated sugar
3 extra-large eggs
1¼ cups heavy cream, 40%
1 ½ teaspoon ground cinnamon
1 teaspoon ground ginger
¼ teaspoon ground nutmeg
¼ teaspoon ground cloves
¼ teaspoon cayenne pepper
¼ teaspoon salt

Preheat oven to 375°. Roll out dough on lightly floured surface to a 12 inch round. Transfer to a 9 inch diameter glass pie dish. Fold overhang under and crimp decoratively. Pierce dough all over with fork. Freeze 15 minutes. Lime crust with foil; fill with dried beans or high weights. Bake until sides are set, about 12 minutes. Remove foil and beans. Reduce oven temperature to 350°. Whisk pumpkin and ¾ cup sugar in large bowl to blend. Whisk in eggs, then cream, spices and salt. Pour filling into warm crust. Bake pie until filling is set in center, about 15 minutes. Transfer pie to cool; cool 30 minutes. Chill until cold, at least 2 hours and up to 1 day. Sprinkle pie evenly with 2 tablespoons sugar. Using propane torch, flame until sugar melts and begins to caramelize, turning pie for even browning, about 1 minute. Let pie stand until topping hardens, about 20 minutes. Sprinkle pie again with remaining 2 tablespoons of sugar. Flame again until sugar browns, about 1 minute. Serves 8.

BANANA CAKE
WITH CINNAMON CARAMEL SAUCE

Cake:
2 cups white flour
1 teaspoon baking soda
½ teaspoon baking powder
½ teaspoon salt
1 cup white granulated sugar
½ cup vegetable oil
1 ½ cup ripe bananas, mashed, about 3 large
2 extra large eggs
½ cup whole milk
1 vanilla bean, split and scrapped

Preheat oven to 350F. Whisk flour, baking soda, baking powder and salt in medium bowl to combine. Whisk sugar and oil in large bowl to blend. Add mashed bananas and eggs and whisk to blend well. Add flour mixture and whisk just until combined. Whisk in milk and vanilla. Divide batter equally among 8 brioche cups. Place on baking sheet, for 25 minutes. Cool slightly.

Sauce:
½ cup white sugar
½ cup brown sugar
½ cup heavy cream, 40%
½ cup unsalted butter
½ teaspoon cinnamon

In a medium sauce pan, combine all ingredients and bring to softball stage. Remove from heat and add ½ teaspoon pure vanilla extract.

SPICED NUTS

1 ½ cup almonds

1 cups walnuts

1 ½ cup cashews

1 cup pecans

2 extra large egg whites

Good pinch of salt

1 cup white granulated sugar

Pinch cayenne pepper to taste

½ cup, 1 stick, unsalted butter

Beat egg whites, salt, sugar, and cayenne until stiff peaks. Fold in nuts. Melt butter in 9 x 13 inch pan. Pour nut mixture on butter and fold in. bake at 325F until nuts are brown and no butter remains. Stir every 10 minutes to prevent sticking. Bake for about 30 minutes. Remove to container while still slightly warm and cover to prevent sticking together.

LaVergne, TN USA
03 April 2010
177984LV00001B

* 9 7 8 1 4 3 8 9 1 7 8 8 7 *